Y0-BSE-200

Wines & Wineries of New South Wales

This book presents for the first time a complete and concise handbook to the wines and wineries of New South Wales. Each winery is classified on a unique five-point scale for both quality and value. A short history introduces each vineyard, then the author James Halliday gives comprehensive notes on the volume, styles and characteristics of the wines made. He also gives the location of the vineyards, the availability of cellar-door sales and tours, and a recommended list of best buys.

Halliday treats every winemaker on his merits, whether he is producing cheaper wines, drink-now styles, or the best vintages in Australia. This is a unique and valuable reference for all wine drinkers, written with Halliday's typical exuberance, honesty and clarity.

JAMES HALLIDAY is one of Australia's best-known wine writers, most recently through his weekly column in *The National Times*. He is also a respected wine judge and a partner in a small, high-quality vineyard, Brokenwood in the Hunter Valley. Three weekends out of four, he departs the large Sydney law firm where he is managing partner and heads happily north to Brokenwood to practise his many talents as planter, pruner, vintner, critic and wine lover.

Halliday's Selection for Top Quality & Value for Money

The wineries that came out absolutely tops for both quality and value for money, winning an AA rating were, in alphabetical order:

* Brokenwood, Lower Hunter
  Huntington Estate, Mudgee
  Lake's Folly, Lower Hunter
  Lindemans, Lower Hunter
  Miramar, Mudgee
  Richmond Estate, Richmond
  Richmond Grove, Upper Hunter
  Robson Vineyard, Lower Hunter
  Rothbury Estate, Lower Hunter
  Tullochs, Lower Hunter
  Tyrrells, Lower Hunter

These were closely followed by Terrace Vale, Chateau Francois, Hermitage Estate, Wyndham Estate, Amberton, Botobolar, Burnbrae, Craigmoor, Drayton's Bellevue, Hungerford Hill, McWilliams MIA, Montrose, San Bernadino and Tamburlaine.

*Len Evans gave Brokenwood its AA rating.

Wines & Wineries of New South Wales

James Halliday

University of Queensland Press

Created and produced by
Mead & Beckett Publishing
139 Macquarie Street Sydney

First published in 1980 by
University of Queensland Press
St Lucia, Queensland

Designed by Barbara Beckett
Typeset by Meredith Trade Lino, Melbourne
Printed and bound by Shanghai Printing Press, Hong Kong

Distributed in the United Kingdom, Europe, the Middle East,
Africa and the Caribbean by Prentice-Hall International,
International Book Distributors Ltd, 66 Wood Lane End,
Hemel Hempstead, Herts, England.

National Library of Australia
Cataloguing-in-Publication data
Halliday, James
  Wines and Wineries of New South Wales
  ISBN 0 7022 1570 8
  1. Wine and wine making — New South Wales.
  I. Title.
663'.2'009944

Contents

Introduction

New South Wales wines come from a rich diversity of sources and this fact may surprise many wine lovers. There is a special magic in the growing of vines and the making of wines which knows no geographic or social barrier. As many vignerons are doctors, farmers, lawyers, scientists and the like, as are formally trained and qualified oenologists. Big companies and weekend vignerons sit cheek by jowl in surprising harmony.

So it is too that vineyards and wineries can be found from one end of the state to the other. The jigsaw puzzle extends from Inverell in the north to Corowa in the extreme south, and from the metropolitan fringes of Sydney to Forbes, Griffith and Buronga in the west. If this were not enough, more than sixty different varieties of grapes are grown and crushed here each year. Little wonder that wines of many colours, every taste and every style are made in New South Wales. The tendency to think in terms of the Hunter Valley alone is a gross and misleading over-simplification.

In 1979 the MIA produced seventy per cent of the State's output. Ten years ago the figure stood at eighty per cent but the vast increase in Hunter Valley plantings has made its mark. The production of Mudgee is still relatively insignificant in terms of quantity, however it is rapidly establishing itself as a consistent producer of first class whites, reds and roses. We shall undoubtedly hear much more of the area in years to come. In 1979 New South Wales contributed just under a quarter of the total Australian crush, with 118,000 tonnes of grapes. Clearly it will never challenge South Australia in terms of quantity, but it offers as much as any State to the wine lover.

I hope that this book will help you find your way through this part of the totally absorbing and ever-enjoyable world of wine.

How to use this book

In reading the detailed notes below on each of the wineries, keep these points in mind. First, prices are in most instances those applying at the time of writing (April–May 1980). In some cases the companies have supplied forward information covering their pricing structure through the remainder of the year. However, because of retail price variation from one State to another (or even between stores) and because of variations between cellar-door and retail costs, prices quoted should be taken as an approximate guide only.

Secondly, many of the individual wines reviewed will no longer be available by the time you need this book. I have nonetheless included precise tasting notes for many of the lesser known wineries because they do give an indication of the winery's overall style and quality. General "winemaker's notes" are, in my view, not terribly useful. The steady improvement in winemaking techniques is producing an increasing continuity in style and quality from one year to the next.

Third, it happens that both 1979 and 1980 produced good-to-great vintages right across Australia. This applies especially to New South Wales, although the quantity of the 1980 Mudgee vintage was reduced by frost and then drought. The Hunter Valley was particularly fortunate, having successive vintages in near-perfect climatic conditions. So if the '79s are not available, despair not: the '80s should be just as good.

Finally, the estimates for cellaring potential are calculated from the date of vintage. They tend to be conservative, particularly for the better whites and reds. Some people think in terms of absolutes, and for two quite separate reasons this is utterly wrong. First, wines do not magically reach a perfect stage of development on one day and on a subsequent day equally magically dissolve into vinegar. Having reached a certain stage of maturity, many red wines then remain basically unchanged for many years. Second, each person must determine what he is looking for in a wine: there is inevitably some trade-off between loss of fruit freshness on the one hand and increase in complexity on the other, as a wine slowly matures. With the very greatest wines one may have the best of both worlds, but by no means always. So if you enjoy clean, fresh, fruity whites and reds, drink them early; if you like the mellow complexity of age, be patient.

The rating code used is:

Quality	*Value for Money*
A = Outstanding	**A** = Exceptional
B = Very good	**B** = Very good
C = Good	**C** = Good
D = Average	**D** = Acceptable
X = Not rated	**X** = Not rated

Vineyard Areas of New South Wales

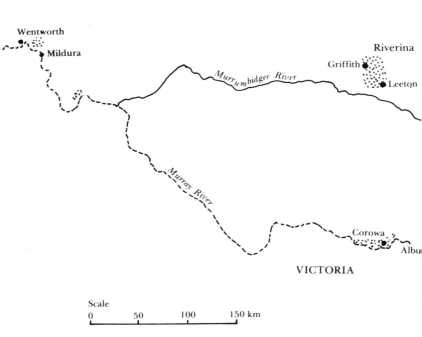

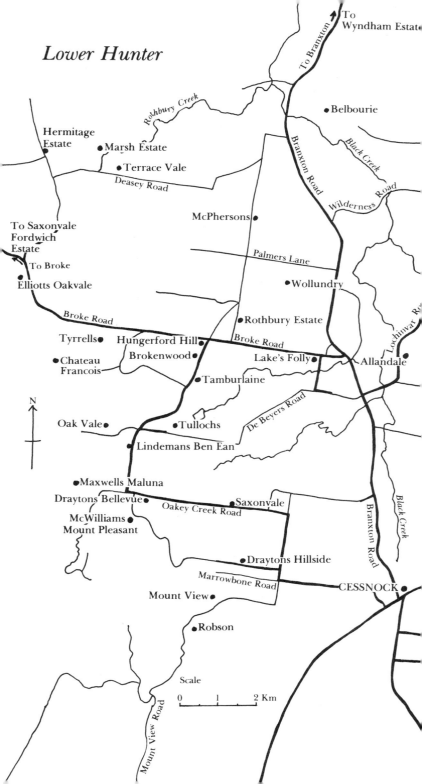

Lower Hunter Valley

The Hunter Valley has a long and proud reputation for producing some of Australia's greatest table wines. After early attempts — some successful, others not — to establish vineyards in and around the fledgling city of Sydney, the centre of viticulture in New South Wales quickly moved to the Hunter Valley.

James Busby's Kirkton vineyard was established in 1824 (under the care of his brother-in-law William Kelman), and by 1832 there were eleven Hunter vineyards — patches of one half to three acres forming only a small part of mixed farming operations.

Growth was steady between 1830 and 1860; from then until the turn of the century was the golden era of the Hunter Valley. Wine made by about twenty vineyards from a myriad varieties (which passed into obscurity for sixty or more years) was exported to other States and the United Kingdom, and was greeted with acclaim in all quarters. Most was dry table wine, but champagne was made by James King of Irrawang over 100 years ago and presented to Napoleon III at the conclusion of the famous 1855 Paris Exhibition. The judges said it had "a bouquet, body and flavour equal to the finest champagne".

From 1900, the Valley went through a process of contraction which continued more or less unabated until 1960. Between 1900 and 1910, hundreds of acres were pulled up as the local winemarket was flooded by cheap imports from South Australia following Federation and the removal of trade barriers. (Those imports were heavily subsidised by the South Australian Government at the point of production.) Many vineyards whose products had been household names in the nineteenth century either reverted to grazing land or were taken over by large companies (often Lindemans).

However, even takeover was no guarantee of survival: Kirkton and Cawarra both went out of production in the twenties and thirties and are retained as brand names only on Lindemans' labels. Catawba, Cote d'or, Bebeah, Kaluda . . . the list of once famous names goes on and on. Even today there are numerous paddocks in which faint ridges and the decayed remnants of end-posts provide proof of once flourishing vineyards.

Concurrent with this contraction in acreage and production was a massive shift in pattern of grape plantings. In the nineteenth century, Chardonnay, Chasselas, Rhine Riesling, Pedro Ximinez, Pinot Noir, Malbec, Petite Verdot and Cabernet Sauvignon were all common varieties. Many others of less importance were also propagated.

By 1956, three varieties — Semillon, Hermitage and White Shiraz — occupied 428 hectares out of the total area of 466 hectares then under vine. By 1977, that area had increased to 4126 hectares, which may prove to be the high point for some years to come. At the end of 1978, the area was down to 3910 hectares, reflecting the chill economic winds which began to blow in the mid '70s as the public turned its back on red wines. Wine companies discovered that merely being present in the Hunter Valley did not give them any divine right to great wine.

The emphasis on those three varieties was influenced by economics and the radically changing tastes of the home and export markets. Fortified wines dominated the market. Not only did they represent almost all our then considerable exports, but also over eighty per cent of all domestic wine sales.

The Hunter continued to make dry table wine because its climate is not as well suited to fortified wines as other major Australian districts. However, no recognition was given on the label to the variety (as there had been in the previous century), and the demand was for robust, high-yielding varieties. This was no economic climate for the delicate, scented Pinot Noir nor the shy bearing Cabernet, and gradually they withered. Thus the wine which prompted the renaissance of Cabernet in the Hunter was made in two hogsheads only. This was a 1930 Wyndham wine, a blend of fifty per cent Cabernet and fifty per cent Petite Verdot. Drunk by Max Lake in the '50s, it was the inspiration for planting Lake's Folly with Cabernet in 1963.

There are now more than twenty varieties grown in significant quantities and an equal number in small or experimental lots. There is now as much Cabernet Sauvignon (462 hectares) as there were total plantings in 1956 — and in that year there was not a single Cabernet vine bearing. The major varieties are Hermitage (1686 hectares), Semillon (993 hectares), Cabernet Sauvignon (462 hectares), Traminer (177 hectares), Rhine Riesling (158 hectares) and Chardonnay (133 hectares).

Against the trend of the past two years (in which plantings of virtually all varieties have been stable or decreasing) plantings of Chardonnay are rapidly increasing, with as many hectares still coming into bearing as are actually producing (66 hectares of each). Lilydale in Victoria, the high hills around Adelaide and the Eden Valley (and elsewhere) may also produce exceptional Chardonnay, but, led by Murray Tyrrell, the Hunter Valley has already proved conclusively that some great wines — by world standards — can be made from this variety.

There is no question that Chardonnay will assume steadily greater importance in the Valley; the only doubt is whether it will ever overtake Semillon. In the very long term, it may conceivably do so, but certainly not in the next thirty or forty years. Semillon produces a very great wine in its own right and healthy bearing vines are not going to be pulled up or grafted to Chardonnay. Any radical re-alignment is far more likely to come from the next cyclic red boom and white-wine glut.

Semillon must have been sired in a climate similar to that of the Hunter, for nowhere else in the world (outside France) does it produce wine of such quality. Even in Australia, it is the poor relation of Rhine Riesling in all regions except the Hunter. There it produces whites which have a capacity to develop and bloom with age in the same way as the Chenin Blanc wines of Vouvray do over thirty, forty or even fifty years.

For many years, Lindemans' Semillon-based Riesling, Chablis and White Burgundies remained unchallenged, but since 1970 a number of remarkable whites have come from new makers both large and small. Rothbury's whites, commencing with the '72 vintage, give every indication of matching Lindemans' stride for stride as the wines from similar vintages from each company slowly mature. The taste and structure of an old Hunter white (say 15 years) is not to everyone's liking. With few exceptions, however, the greater the depth of the wine knowledge of the taster, the more likely it is that he or she will understand and love the wines.

Production of red and white wine was evenly poised in the 1979 vintage: 12,123 tonnes of red compared with 11,291 tonnes of white. Hermitage accounted for a massive 8790 tonnes of total red production, and is obviously destined to be the mainstay for many years. Yet it showed a marked decrease in the twelve-month period from 31 December 1977 to 31 December 1978 from 1908 hectares down to 1686 hectares. I have little doubt that a similar decrease will be recorded for the ensuing twelve months.

It would be wrong, however, to interpret this as an indictment of the quality of Hermitage — part of the decrease is due to a realisation that under irrigated conditions in the Upper Hunter, Hermitage over-crops and can produce a poor wine; part is due to the general surplus of red wine which is limited neither to variety nor district.

Hermitage does produce wines of marvellous softness, warmth and subtlety in the Lower Hunter, which acquire great elegance with sufficient bottle age. Lindemans have finally released their superb 1959 vintage Bin 1590 from show duties (where it won many gold medals and trophies); at $27.50 a bottle it is an outstanding example of Hunter Hermitage at its greatest, and is worth every cent.

However, Cabernet Sauvignon is closing the gap fast — 2777 tonnes were harvested during the 1979 vintage, and it has many advantages in the uncertain Hunter Valley climate. Not the least of these lie in its small berry-size and thick skin, ideal weapons to combat the excess water loosed on the vines by both God and man. Its flavour and colour stand up both to irrigation and to the frequent wet and mouldy vintages which bedevil the district.

Lake's Folly is widely accepted as producing the classic Hunter Cabernets, but a number of other vineyards, particularly the small ones, produce wines of very good and at times equal quality. Despite the recent staggering success of Murray Tyrrell's Pinot Noir in Paris against some of the greatest wines of the world, I have doubts about the long-term worth of this variety. It may be that the clones so far employed are inferior, but for my money there is simply inadequate flavour, colour and, above all, true varietal character in the wines. Given the abysmal yields (seldom more than three tonnes per hectare), it becomes a highly unattractive proposition.

The capacity of the Hunter to produce truly great wines from all these varieties, and a host of others, proves once again that the vine flourishes best under adversity. Much of the soil is poor, the day-degree-summation (overall measure of heat) is far too high, and vintage-time rain much too prevalent. However, each of these clouds has its silver lining: poor soil is frequently capable of producing finer wine than rich soil; the cloud cover which sometimes produces rain also reduces moisture-loss and stress, thereby significantly offsetting the effects of heat.

The interplay of these and other factors would be the subject of a book themselves, and outside the scope of this brief introduction. Suffice it to say that in every vintage there are wines made somewhere in the Hunter which can stand up in competition with the best France, California or any other wine district or nation can offer.

The Allandale Winery

There were plenty of knockers when Ed Jouault established Allandale in 1978: stories — no doubt apocryphal — of Jouault with winemaking text-book in one hand and crusher controls in the other. Such people have vanished now; instead, there are queues at Allandale winery in the weekend seeking the interesting small parcels of wine (each release seldom exceeds 500 dozen) made by Allandale from its bought-in grapes.

Allandale, alone in the Hunter, relies solely on purchased material, having no vineyards of its own. There are great advantages in such a system, particularly when as at the moment there is a grape surplus. Jouault is clearly obtaining high-quality fruit and treating it with considerable skill.

Modern equipment and Jouault's wide understanding of wine in all its facets (he won the 1979 Vin de Champagne Award to study in Champagne during that vintage) combine to produce wines of good-to-excellent quality.

Established: 1978.

Address: Allandale Road, Pokolbin via Maitland 2321, 5 kms north of Cessnock (049) 904526.

Winemaker: Ed Jouault.

Annual crush: 70–80 tonnes bought in.

Principal wines/wine styles

Small parcels in the 250–650 dozen range identifying both the variety and vineyard.

Semillons: The accent is on fresh fruit, brilliantly clear green/gold colour, with the acid balance necessary to ensure long life. Variety offered in steel, French and German oak-matured wines from various vineyards.

Chardonnay: Will sell out immediately on release. Jouault is a good enough winemaker to bring out the best from this marvellous variety.

Shiraz: Various styles on offer ranging from light to medium full-bodied. The wines have a good colour and fruit flavours stemming from low pH and good acid.

Cabernet Sauvignon: An excellent '79 Cabernet was made from grapes grown on the Leonard estate showing intense Cabernet flavour and with very good balance.

Fleur: A very interesting, late picked, sweet white made from a veritable fruit salad of Semillon, Traminer and Chardonnay.

Best Buys

1979 Leonard Semillon: $3.00

1979 Fleur: $3.50

1979 Leonard Cabernet Sauvignon: Price not available at time of writing; release due at or about publication date.

15

Cellaring potential: White wines (Semillon and Chardonnay) 3–7+years;
Shiraz 4–6 years; Cabernet Sauvignon 5–8+ years.
Cellar door sales/facilities: Open Monday to Saturday 9 am to 5 pm. Sunday 12 noon to 5 pm. Full tasting facilities.
Retail distribution: Virtually all wines sold cellar door or by mailing list; inquiries welcome.
Summary: High-quality wines made in very small quantities and offering an impressive choice to the most fastidious of wine buyers.

CD Belbourie

Jim Roberts, the owner–winemaker of Belbourie, marches to a different drum. Intensely individualistic, he is at once a master showman–salesman and an introvert moving uneasily in the company of his fellows.

This split personality manifests itself in his wines and wine-making practices. Fifteen years ago he was using techniques such as carbonic maceration for reds and new wood maturation for whites, which are only now being employed by other and better known wineries in the Valley. He was one of the very first to plant exotic varieties for commercial production and used a 'moon buggy' mobile crusher allowing grapes to be crushed in the vineyard under a protective blanket of CO_2.

Having taken pains to eliminate oxidation, he then subjects the wines to a prolonged solera-type wood-ageing process involving a blending of a number of vintages as wine is progressively removed for bottling and fresh wine added to the partially empty cask.The date of the Belah (white) and Bungan (red) ranges denotes simply the year of bottling. "78" Belah contains wine from the four vintages, '76–79, with an average age of two-and-a-half years.

The wines so produced are unlike any others made in the Hunter Valley. Carrodus of Yarra Yering, Victoria and Tom Brodoghy of County Hamley are the only 'relatives'. If you are prepared to accept oxidation, volatility and massive oak flavours as the price of overall immense flavour, Belbourie wines are for you.

Established: 1964.

Address: Branxton Road, Rothbury, 24 kilometres north of Cessnock. (049) 38 1556.

Winemaker: Jim Roberts.

Annual crush: 50–60 tonnes.

Principal wines/wine styles

Belah 78–79: Heavy oak, strong volatility, deep colour, noticeable oxidation and immense flavour of great appeal to a limited but fanatically loyal section of the public.

Super Belah 76–79: All the above, only more so. A quite incredible wine which has no parallel in Australia (or elsewhere, for that matter).

Hermitage – Carbonic Maceration: Intense flavour with all manner of esters and nuances, but volatile to the end.

Light Bungan: Wild flavour with possibly the highest level of volatility I have ever encountered in a commercial wine.

Best buys: Strictly a matter of preference. Prices range from $5.00 to $7.50 a bottle for members of the public and $3.50 to $4.50 for club members.

Retail distribution: Nil; all wine sold cellar door and by mail order to Belbourie Subscription Club members. Inquiries welcome.

Summary: High-priced wines attractively presented, which allow no compromise; you will either love them or hate them.

Brokenwood

Owned and run by a small syndicate of which the author was a founding partner, Brokenwood is and always will be a red-wine vineyard (despite a few acres of Chardonnay planted in 1980).

Cabernet Sauvignon, Hermitage, Pinot Noir and Malbec

(plus a little Cabernet Franc and Merlot) are planted on tough, red-clay soils producing very low yields of high-quality grapes. Early picking; controlled fermentation in stainless steel tanks with hand plunging; maturation in new, small Nevers oak casks; bottling after ten or eleven months in cask and a dislike of H_2S — all these result in wines with deeper and more stable colour, fresher fruit and better balance when young than many other reds of the district. The wines nonetheless age well, with only the '73 vintage (Brokenwood's first, and from eighteen-month-old vines) showing signs of being fully ready to drink.

Until the '78 vintage, restricted output resulted in all wines being sold privately. Since then increased output has allowed wider distribution, and the wines have received considerable praise from wine writers and a high level of success from the limited show entries the vineyard is able to make in national shows. The '75 Cabernet was judged the top wine in a masked tasting by a number of Australia's top wine judges against the best of France, California and Australia that year.

Established: 1970.
Address: McDonalds Road, Pokolbin, 2321, 11 km north-west of Cessnock. (049) 987 559.
Winemaker(s): John Beeston, James Halliday, Nick Bulleid with a lot of help from six other syndicate members.
Annual crush: 35–40 tonnes (30 tonnes estate grown; 6 tonnes bought in).
Annual sales: 2200 Cases.
Principal wines/wine styles
Cabernet Sauvignon: Extremely long-lived wines with strong varietal character in the austere, cool climate mould. Need at least 8 years to develop and soften.
Hermitage Cabernet: Beautifully coloured, totally clean wine (100% Hunter) with approximately 60% Hermitage. Fruit, oak, acid and tannin balance usually very good. Very attractive when young but will repay long cellaring.
Cabernet Hermitage: Hunter–Coonawarra blend with 30% Coonawarra Cabernet (total Cabernet 60% approximately) giving lifted fresh berry flavour and again showing no traditional Hunter character whatsoever. Long-lived but also seductive when young.
Pinot Hermitage: Made in very small quantities. The '76 vintage won the trophy for best small-maker red at the Hunter Valley Wine Show in 1977. Strawberry Pinot flavour lifts and lightens Hermitage.
Hermitage: A straight hermitage is made only in exceptional years. The '79 was a marvellous wine.

18

```
┌─────────────────────────────┐  ┌─────────────────────────────┐
│             1979            │  │             1973            │
│      BROKENWOOD            │  │      BROKENWOOD            │
│  hermitage, cabernet sauvignon │  │    cabernet sauvignon      │
│                             │  │                             │
│  mcdonalds road, pokolbin, n.s.w. │  │ pokolbin road, pokolbin, n.s.w. │
│  738 ml:      produce of australia │  │ 738 ml:      produce of australia │
└─────────────────────────────┘  └─────────────────────────────┘
```

Best buys
Only two wines remain available:
Hermitage Cabernet 1979: $4.00
Cabernet Hermitage (Hunter–Coonawarra) 1979: $4.00
(Prices cellar door current to December 1980)
Cellaring potential: Cabernet: 5–15+ years; Cabernet
Hermitage blends: 3–8+ years; Hermitage Pinot blends:
3–5+ years.
Retail distribution: Sold principally ex-vineyard (mail orders–
inquiries welcome to Box 1107, GPO Sydney), but also sold by
more than 20 fine wine outlets in Sydney, and a limited number
in Melbourne, Adelaide, Perth and Hobart.
Summary: High-quality, Cabernet-based wines which show
vineyard rather than regional character, and which develop
considerable complexity with age while still holding fruit
flavour and strong red-purple colour.

Chateau Francois

Chateau Francois nestles under the very brow of the Brokenback Range with its tiny plantings running down the flanks of
the foothills. It is as hard to find (a dirt track through a grazing
paddock) as its wines, but both are well worth the search. Indeed, the output is so small that owner–winemaker Don Francois neither opens to the public for tasting nor sells any wine
through retail channels. All is sold (quickly) through its private
mail-order list.

The quick sales are not surprising, for Francois must be the
most successful small exhibitor in Australian wine shows for the
past twenty years at least. He makes clean, full-flavoured Semillons which are immensely attractive at two or three years of age
(but which will hold longer, of course), and a number of elegant
medium-bodied Shiraz and Shiraz Pinot reds.

Although strictly a weekend winemaker (he is the Director of
Fisheries for New South Wales, hence the trout on his label) he
takes immense care with his wines and I have no doubt this
constant vigilance has much to do with the quality of the product.

Established: 1970.

Address: Broke Road, Pokolbin, 13 km north-west of Cessnock (040) 987549.

Winemaker: Don Francois.

Annual crush: 8–10 tonnes estate grown.

Principal wines/wine styles

1978 Semillon: Winner of 2 gold, 2 silver and one bronze medal at the 1978–79 Hunter Valley, Mudgee and National Wine Shows, with trophy in Class 3 at 1979 Hunter Valley Show. Extremely smooth, clean wine with full Semillon fruit flavour and a long but fairly soft finish. Deserves its success.

1977 Shiraz: A vintage which produced some remarkably full-flavoured and deep-coloured reds. The wine retains the Francois stamp of elegance, but is a little fuller and firmer than some of his wines.

1977 Shiraz–Pinot Noir: An exceptionally attractive wine with real Pinot Noir flavour of the authentic sappy kind evident, although married with the richer flavour of the Hermitage.

Best buys

1978 Semillon: $3.50

1977 Shiraz: $3.00

1977 Shiraz–Pinot Noir: $3.50

(prices for July 1980 release of these wines)

Cellaring potential: Semillon, 3–6+ years; Shiraz, 4–7 years; Shiraz Pinot Noir, 4–6 years.

Cellar door sales/facilities: Open by arrangement only; inquiries to vineyard. Mail-order inquiries to winery or to 8 Stafford Street, Paddington, 2021.

Retail distribution: Nil.

Summary: One of Australia's smallest wineries offering wine to the public but which makes up for what it lacks in quantity by excellent quality. Outstanding value for money.

Draytons "Bellevue"

Others come and go with fashions changing overnight, but the Drayton family continues quietly making wine much the same way as their forebears have for the past 100 years. They and Tyrrells are the only two survivors of the founding wine families who continue to own and operate their own businesses.

Draytons' business may not have increased dramatically as Tyrrells', but it is nonetheless a very different operation from that of 15 years ago. There are now five estates owned either by the company or by members of the family: Bellevue, Lambkin, Ivanhoe, Pokolbin Hills and Mangerton. These are all identified on current labels, but significant quantities of varietal wines are also released, made from the sixty per cent of the total crush coming from outside growers.

Much of Draytons' output is sold cellar door and through outlets in the Newcastle area. Distribution in the remainder of New South Wales and Victoria has always been patchy and so the wines are not as well known as they deserve to be.

The white wines have a peculiar, tart-apple character reminiscent of those of McWilliams, and unlike any other makers. This applies particularly to the Semillon and Rhine Riesling. More conventional Traminer Riesling is made, and in 1979 and 1980 a quite outstanding Chardonnay. The reds show distinct vintage variation, as much because of cellar practices as the vagaries of the Hunter climate. At their best they offer exceptional value for money.

Established: 1860.

Address: Oakey Creek Road, Cessnock, 2321, 7 km west of Cessnock (049) 987 513.

Winemaker: Reg and Trevor Drayton.

Annual crush: 600 tonnes.

Principal wines/winestyles

Chardonnay: A new venture for Draytons but greeted with immediate success. After a low-profile start in 1978, marvellous wines were made in 1979 and 1980 from grapes grown on the Mangerton vineyard. The wine is matured in German oak, which gives it a style quite distinct from the more commonly encountered French (Tyrrells) and American wood used elsewhere.

Semillon: Different in style and structure from all other Hunter whites (except McWilliams), sometimes matured in large old oak and sometimes in steel but always exhibiting a full appley flavour and having a composition which holds them together for many years. The '77 is a trophy winner.

Rhine Riesling: Has a character all its own. Extremely long-lived

— more than any other N.S.W. Rhine. At 7 to 10 years of age is a marvellous wine. The '66 vintage is still at the top of its form.

Ivanhoe Hermitage: Shows some new oak influence and can be extremely good (the '75 was outstanding).

Bellevue Hermitage: Less oak and more depth to the fruit, but sometimes a little straightforward. The '75 was also outstanding.

Cabernet Hermitage: Over the years, since the '67, has produced some of Draytons' finest reds, equal to the Hunter's best. Has greater strength and complexity than most of the other reds in the Draytons' stable.

Fortified Wines: A full range is available, much of it bought in from other makers.

Best buys

Chardonnay 1979 (or 1980): $3.00

Semillon 1977 Bin 7717: $2.55

Bellevue Cabernet Hermitage 1977: $3.20

Cellaring potential: Semillon 2 to 7 years; Rhine Riesling and Chardonnay 3 to 10 years; Hermitage 3 to 5 years; Cabernet Hermitage 4 to 8+ years.

Cellar door sales/facilities: Open Monday to Saturday 7 am to 5 pm. Tasting and BBQ facilities. Limited fast foods available.

Retail distribution: Distribution by Cinzano throughout New South Wales, and Rhinecastle in Victoria. Cellar-door and mail-order sales welcome.

Summary: Generally underrated (the reds particularly). Draytons offers a cross-section of traditionally made Hunter wines at very competitive prices.

XX Elliotts Wines

The old-established and highly respected family winery and business of Doug Elliott was one of the major casualties in the Hermitage Estate receivership. As a result of a complicated series of sales, defaults, repurchases and spin offs the old winery has been transferred back to Doug and John Elliott; the Tallawanta vineyard sold to a group of Cessnock businessmen, and the Fordwich Estate to interests associated with Len Evans. The Elliott family continues to own (as it has always done) the Belford vineyard and will market under a new Oak Vale label. The brand name Elliotts Wines has remained with Wyndham.

The wines still on sale were made before the disintegration of the Elliotts' structure. It is unlikely that Wyndham will let the name die, and if its previous marketing strategy is any guide we will see the future development of specialised styles for release under the Elliott label.

Established: 1893.

Annual sales: 5000 Cases.

Principal wines/wine styles

As at May 1980 the following wines were still available:

Hunter Spatlese Riesling 1978: $2.95

Hunter White Burgundy 1978: $2.95

Hunter Semillon Chardonnay 1978: $2.95

Hunter Cabernet Shiraz 1975: $2.95

Summary: A once great Hunter vineyard name now in a state of limbo.

Hermitage Estate

Hermitage Estate is yet another of a group of flamboyant wineries which I once described as Boomtime Babies. And like many of its sisters, it soon ran into financial difficulty and ultimately a lengthy period of receivership. With no real prospects of trading out, it was inevitable that it would join the Wyndham camp, a marriage consummated in 1978. For a number of years before and during the receivership, a considerable portion of Wyndham's crush had been carried out at Hermitage. The capacity of the winery was predicated on the assumption that all of the 300 hectares would produce the same quantity as the initial 80 hectares at Mistletoe Farm. This proved false and most of the vineyard was uneconomic.

It has now shrunk back to 80 hectares and the vast capacity of the winery is utilised by processing most of the Wyndham material as well as making bulk wine for other companies.

In preparing the notes on Wyndham I commented on the extraordinary colour and fruit flavour of the red wines. Hermitage has two of the three Rotatank Fermenters in Australia (the other is at Leo Burings). These hold 36 tonnes of grapes and revolve on a huge lateral axle. The revolution speed is adjustable, and the tank is able to extract enormous colour and flavour. Winemaker Neil McGuigan (younger brother of Brian McGuigan) has obviously got it down to a fine art.

Established: 1967.

Address: Deasey Road, Pokolbin, 15 km north of Cessnock (049) 987 578.

Winemaker: Neil McGuigan.

Annual crush: 1,900 tonnes.

Annual sales: 5,000 cases.

RHINE RIESLING 1979

This limited release of our 1979 Rhine Riesling was made from selected Rhine fruit; the fruit was harvested and processed with ultimate care to produce a wine of considerable flavour and delicacy.
A delight to consume with seafoods now, but will continue to develop into a White Burgundy wine in years to come.

PRODUCE OF AUSTRALIA 750ml
HERMITAGE WINES LTD   POKOLBIN   HUNTER VALLEY   NEW SOUTH WALES
D/3251

Principal wines/wine styles

Limited Release Traminer Riesling 1979: cold fermentation, the judicious retention of sugar, and the well proven combination of the crisp acid Rhine Riesling with the soft and aromatic Traminer result in an easy drinking, flavoursome and highly commercial style.

Limited Release Semillon 1976: Limited stocks of this golden, beautifully mature white still remain at bargain prices of $2.95.

Limited Release Semillon Chardonnay 1978: Another wine with considerable bottle development and again a bargain.

Trophy Cabernet Sauvignon 1978: Exceptional colour, deep and intense. Fruit/alcohol on nose suggests fairly ripe material. Considerable varietal flavour is married with American oak and leads on to a full bodied finish with considerable tannin. The winner of 2 trophies and 3 gold medals.

Gold Medal Shiraz 1978: Extraordinary inky-blue colour. High alcohol wine. Dense wine of huge flavour and utterly atypical of conventional Hunter reds.

Best buys

Limited Release Semillon 1976: $2.95

Limited Release Semillon Chardonnay 1978: $2.95

Trophy Cabernet Sauvignon 1978: $4.15

Gold Medal Shiraz 1978: $3.75

Cellaring potential: Aromatic whites 1–2 years; Semillon and Chardonnay 3–6 years; reds 5–9 years.

Cellar door sales/facilities: Open Monday to Saturday 10 am to 5 pm; Sunday noon to 5 pm. Full tasting facilities; BBQs; Johnnie Walker's Restaurant in the Hunter. Cellar door sales welcome.

Retail distribution: Limited New South Wales.

Summary: As with Hollydene, the company is taking a very low profile until the problems associated with its receivership are forgotten. The wines are sold under the Hunter Valley Estate label.

X Honeytree Vineyard

One of the least known vineyards in the Hunter, as its wines have not previously been on offer to visitors. Owner Maurice Schlesinger expects to obtain a licence by July 1980.

The 24 acre vineyard is planted to Semillon, Traminer, Blanquette, Cabernet and Hermitage. There is no winery and Schlesinger has the wine made for him. In 1976 and 1977 this was done by Murray Tyrrell; in 1978 Ed Jouault of Allandale made and sold all the wine; in 1979 Hungerford Hill made the wine; and in 1980, Rosemount Estate — an arrangement which Schlesinger hopes will continue until he builds his own winery.

Established: 1973.

Address: Gillards Road, Pokolbin, 14 km north west of Cessnock. (02) 273541.

Winemaker: Rosemount Estate Pty Limited.

Principal wines/wine styles

Hermitage 1976: Excellent colour. Rich, strong spicy Rhone style bouquet and similar palate. Lots of flavour in an impressive and different style (50 dozen available at time of writing).

Cabernet Sauvignon 1976. Fruity, generous style reminiscent of some Californian Cabernets. Camphor oak married with fruit flavour and a hint of the same spice as in the Hermitage (50 dozen available).

Semillon 1979: Strong, almost viscous fruit flavour on palate. Distinct SO_2 on bouquet which will hopefully dissipate with age. (1000 cases).

Best buys: All wines, including upcoming '79 Cabernet and '79 Shiraz, which will be priced at approximately $3.00 a bottle.

Cellar door sales/facilities: When licence is given open Monday to Saturday 9 am to 5 pm; Sunday noon to 5 pm.

Retail distribution: Camperdown Cellars, Sydney.

Summary: Not rated because of lack of uniformity in winemakers, but if the 76 reds are any guide, the vineyard is capable of producing very high quality fruit.

AB Hungerford Hill

Hungerford Hill was one of the numerous children of the wine boom of the late '60s, and in common with all the others, found the '70s a difficult and hostile environment. It has survived, toughened and trimmed in size (from 235 hectares of vines down to 116) and is undoubtedly here to stay.

For some obscure reason, the Hungerford Hill collection-label reds and whites have never received the recognition they deserve. The principal white is of course made from Semillon, fresh and delicate when young, but with the capacity to develop into a wine ranking with the very best the district can produce (witness the '73 and '75 wines). Some very attractive Traminer Rieslings have been made, but I have the feeling that Hungerford Hill is yet to unlock the secret of getting the best out of its Chardonnay.

The reds are more broadly based in quality, with a Cabernet Sauvignon, a Hermitage and a Cabernet Malbec all offering positive varietal characteristics and a greater depth of colour and flavour than many of their competitors.

The Hungerford Hill village deserves a special mention as one of the foremost scenic attractions of the Hunter Valley. Blending naturally into the spotted gums which abound on the natural slope, it offers something for everyone.

Established: 1967.

Address: Cnr. Broke Road & McDonalds Road, Pokolbin, 11 km north-west of Cessnock. (049) 987 519.

Winemaker: Heydon Osborne.

Annual crush: 1000 tonnes, estate grown.

Annual sales: 56,000 cases.

Principal wines/wine styles

Collection Semillon: One of the slow-developing Hunter styles

which borders on the innocuous when young but builds up colour and honeyed flavour over about 5 years. The '79 tends to prove the exception, being remarkably complete and round at 15 months of age.

Collection Gewurztraminer: One of the lighter styles and usually available only in restricted quantities. One or two vintages have developed exceptional flavour in bottle.

Collection Chardonnay: A range that has so far been extremely disappointing.

Collection Shiraz: A grossly underrated line, with far more depth and strength to its structure and colour than many of the district's reds. Occasionally a whiff of H_2S intrudes, but typically the wines are very clean, with good fruit.

Collection Cabernet Sauvignon: Undoubtedly one of the better Cabernets in the Hunter Valley. Good colour, nice balance, oak held in restraint, with good varietal definition.

Collection Cabernet Malbec: Released only at cellar door, with immense colour and flavour.

Collection Pinot Noir: Above-average colour and flavour. Also available cellar door only.

Best buys
Collection Semillon '79: $3.65
Collection Cabernet Sauvignon: $4.22
Collection Cabernet Malbec: $4.22

Cellaring potential: Semillon 3–5 + years; Shiraz 3–5+ years; Cabernet 4–7+ years.

Cellar door sales/facilities: Open Monday to Saturday, 8.30 am to 5 pm; Sunday 12 noon to 5 pm. The most comphrensive tasting–tourist–restaurant–picnic facilities of any winery in Australia.

Retail distribution: National, but special cellar-door lines and sales an attraction.

Summary: Hungerford Hill produces wines of a high standard, offering above-average cellaring potential. The deep-coloured reds are the most underrated wines now produced in the Hunter Valley.

AA Lake's Folly

It is a little short of extraordinary that such a small vineyard with inevitably limited output should be a household name in Australia and be featured (for example) on the wine list at The Ritz Hotel, London. Perhaps the size — intellectual and physical — of its owner–winemaker, Dr Max Lake, is sufficient explanation.

Dr Lake re-established Cabernet Sauvignon in the Valley in 1963, so it is hardly surprising that Cabernet forms the basis of the vineyard's red-wine production. Two reds are released: a straight Cabernet, and Lake's Folly Dry Red. The latter is a blend of Cabernet and Hermitage with a little Merlot thrown in from time to time.

Extended wood maturation adds considerable complexity; I have not shared in the near-universal adulation of all of the older vintages, but the '77 and '78 Cabernets are quite outstanding wines.

More recently, Lake has turned his attention to Chardonnay and, in the winter of '79, substantially increased his hitherto tiny plantings of this variety. The character and structure of the Chardonnays so far produced has varied considerably from heavy, oak-rich styles to the Corton-like austerity and acidity of the yet-to-be-released '79.

Established: 1963.
Address: Broke Road, Pokolbin, 2321, 8 km north of Cessnock. (049) 987 507.
Winemakers: Max and Stephen Lake.
Annual crush: 35 tonnes.
Annual sales: 2700 cases.
Principal wines/wine styles
Folly Red: A blend of Cabernet and Hermitage (dominant), Malbec and a little Merlot. Elegant wines, with beautifully handled oak. The only criticism is that some have a trace of H_2S, something which others simply see as a function of district character and indeed an integral part of desirable Hunter flavour and structure.
Cabernet Sauvignon: Lake's Cabernets have a style and structure all of their own, which is only fitting, and that extra edge of elegance, and for me at least, that edge of H_2S. But the more recent vintages have been marvellous, and I just wonder whether there have been a few winemaking changes co-inciding

with the arrival of Stephen Lake and the departure (from the winery) of Andy Philips. The '78 in particular is magnificent, utterly clean and showing sweeter oak than the earlier years. I have a personal soft spot for the '77.

Chardonnay: Max Lake has put an immense amount of effort into his Chardonnay. It is so hard to come by and my judgment is not based on wide experience, but I cannot accept that they are the greatest wines made in Australia, as some would have it. Some day they may be.

Best buys
Cabernet Sauvignon 1979: $5.00
Chardonnay 1980 (if you can find it).

Cellaring potential: Folly Red 3–6 years; Cabernet 4–8 years; Chardonnay 4–7 years.

Cellar door facilities: Lake imports a little piece of Ireland to the Hunter by letting it be known he is open for tasting and sales when the gates are open.

Retail distribution: Virtually nil: Camperdown Cellars, Sydney occasionally have a few bottles.

Summary: Hand-crafted, eagerly sought-after and not inexpensive wines from a most gifted winemaker who is a legend in his own lifetime.

Lindemans Wines

If I were asked to nominate a single winery which regularly produces the best Hunter wines, there would be only one possible choice: Lindemans. Furthermore, if I had to justify the assertion that Hunter Semillon needs ten years and Hunter Hermitage fifteen years to show their best, Lindemans would be my star witness.

Since the 1930s, Lindemans has produced a seemingly endless stream of superb wines, both red and white. Because of a farsighted marketing policy, it is possible to purchase dry reds from the 1959 vintage and onwards; dry whites from '61 vintage onwards; sweet whites from '56 on. The prices are high but the wines are impressive.

If you really want to understand what fully mature and great wines of the Hunter are all about, buy a 1961 Bin 1616 Semillon, a 1959 Bin 1590 Burgundy and a '56 Bin 1290 Porphyry. You will not have much change left out of $100, but in terms of great wine you will have had full value.

In the final analysis, the quality and character of the whites are greater than the reds. Throughout the '60s, the company produced a range of whites which are still readily available on retail shelves, and which stretch the complexity, richness and subtlety of Hunter Semillon to the limit. Green-golden in colour, with an aroma of dark toast and a honeyed-nut flavour, they are classic wines which at times merge utterly with great White Burgundies (French, that is).

The reds are velvet smooth, low in tannin, long in flavour, and with complexity added by a curious but far from unpleasant amalgam of a trace of volatility and a trace of H_2S, which is Lindemans' stamp. Someone once described it as a hint of cabbage, and, if that is not taken unkindly, it is not a bad description.

Established: 1870.
Address: McDonalds Road, Pokolbin, 2321, 9 km north-west of Cessnock. (049) 987501.
Winemaker: Chris Buring.
Annual crush: 1000 tonnes.
Principal wines/wine styles:
Hunter River Riesling: A not-terribly-clear description of a Semillon which is in between a Chablis and a white Burgundy in style. These are wines which usually show virtually nothing when first

Lindemans
1975
HUNTER RIVER
BURGUNDY
BIN 5103
LINDEMANS WINES PTY. LTD. SYDNEY
PRODUCE OF 750 ml AUSTRALIA

Lindemans
1979
HUNTER RIVER
RIESLING
BIN 5655
LINDEMANS WINES PTY. LTD. SYDNEY
PRODUCE OF 750 ml AUSTRALIA

released, although vintages such as '79 prove the exception by offering much even when young. The fresh and delicate 2-year-old wines often go through an ugly phase 5 or 6 years after vintage as they develop the golden colour and deep honeyed palate of the mature wine.

Hunter River Chablis: Always exhibits a greater acidity than the two other principal styles, and for this reason can be quite magnificent with age. The '68 Bin 3475 is still developing and has at least another 5 years in front of it. Wines which at all stages of their life have a great deal of finesse.

Hunter River White Burgundy: Deepest and often the quickest maturing of the trio of whites. Deep golden colour with age and tremendous structure.

Chardonnay: Apart from the isolated release in the late '60s, a new development for Lindemans. A very good '79 is in the pipeline.

Verdelho: An occasional release, with a superb '68 on sale within the past two years.

Hunter River Burgundy: All Hermitage-based with the occasional drop of Pinot Noir. Remarkable range, with three releases from each vintage ranging from light to full bodied. Lindemans have the ability to produce top wines in mediocre years. All share great elegance and smoothness.

Best buys
Bin 77 White Burgundy: (blend of many districts): $2.75
Hunter River Chardonnay Bin 5688, 1979 $4.80
Hunter River White Burgundy Bin 5670 1979: $4.10
Hunter River Burgundy Bin 3300 1966: $9.50
Hunter River Burgundy Bin 5103 1975: $4.25

Cellaring potential: Semillons, 4 to 20+ years; Hermitage, 6 to 20+ years.

Cellar door sales/facilities: Open Monday to Saturday, 9 am to 4.30 pm. Winery tours Monday to Friday 11 am to 2.30 pm.

Retail distribution: National; top wines through Lindemans classic wine stockists.

Summary: The classic white and red styles of the Hunter, often seductive when young but developing gloriously when given time in bottle. Both current and old vintages are readily available, providing an instant cellar for the newcomer or treasures for the wine buff.

McPhersons Wines

At the time of writing, McPhersons — or the Pokolbin Co-operative Limited, to give its correct name — is facing severe financial difficulties, and its future is far from clear. Founded around a co-operative of ten vineyards, unconventional thinking has always been a feature of the operation. Not only was a wide variety of unusual grape types planted — McPhersons releases the only Marsanne (white) and Blue Imperial or Cinsault (red) wines from the Hunter — but the winery relies extensively on gravity-flow systems rather than pumps.

Wine quality has tended to be variable, but never lacking in interest. By May 1980, only two of the eight '79 white releases had not sold out, and none of the three '78 red releases remained available. So if the rumours are true, it certainly was not due to lack of popularity of the wines.

Established: 1968.

Address: McDonalds Road, Pokolbin, 11 km north-west of Cessnock. (049) 987 585.

Winemaker: Andrew McPherson.

Annual crush: 530 tonnes.

Principal wines/wine styles

Varietals released include Bin 54 Chenin Blanc; Bin 59 Chardonnay; Bin 58 Sauvignon Blanc; Bin 53 Marsanne; Bin 52 Traminer; Bin 51 Traminer Riesling; Bin 60 Moselle; Bin 40 Blue Imperial; Bin 60 Cabernet Shiraz; Bin 67 Cabernet Sauvignon; Bin 65 Shiraz Mataro; Bin 70 Vintage Port.

The '79 Chardonnay was quite simply a poor wine with strong H_2S flattening the wine and stripping it of flavour. The Marsanne '79 was an entirely different story: considerable residual sugar but excellent fruit flavour and would clearly be a highly successful commercial style.

Best buys: Marsanne Bin 53: $3.15

Cabernet Sauvignon Bin 67: $3.15

Cellaring potential: Aromatic white styles, 1—2 years; reds, 4—5 years.

Cellar door sales/facilities: Open Monday to Saturday 9 am to 5 pm; Sunday noon to 5 pm. Full tasting facilities.

Retail distribution: Limited, but includes Great Australian Wine Company, 35a Willoughby Road, Crows Nest, Sydney. Principal sales cellar door/mail order. Inquiries welcome.
Summary: A winery which has always offered alternative styles and varieties.

McWilliams Wines

Next after Lindemans, McWilliams would have the greatest reputation in the Hunter. Regrettably, it is increasingly a question of how far that reputation is founded on past glories rather than present realities.

Until 1956, a succession of great wines were made by the legendary Maurice O'Shea. Since that time an unmistakeable tarry character — quite certainly an H_2S derivative — has crept into the reds. With the exceptional fruit of the special bins (Robert, OP, OH and the like) some of the wines have sufficient character and flavour to carry what I can only regard as a disability. But the standard commercial lines such as Philip Hermitage cannot cope with it; the '74 Philip should never have been released under the Mt Pleasant label. I hope it represented a low point in a once illustrious range, but one which did not produce anything acceptable from 1969 until the '75.

Several Pinot Hermitage blends have been excellent; the '65 was outstanding, and the '66, '67 and '70 vintages very good. The most recently released (the '72) was a disaster. The white wines, headed by Anne and Elizabeth Riesling are much better. Neither are classic Hunters, having a distinctive appley tang and seldom developing the rich honeyed flavour of Lindemans. But Elizabeth Riesling provides a safe haven in the stormy seas of many a restaurant wine list; while Anne Riesling is one of the longest lived of all Hunter white styles.

Established: 1880.
Address: Marrowbone Road, Pokolbin 2321, 7 km west of Cessnock. (049) 987 505.
Winemaker: Brian Walsh.
Annual Crush: 1500 tonnes.
Principal wines/wine styles
Elizabeth Riesling: Probably the top selling Hunter Semillon, very well made and always of reliable quality. Not really classic in style, but enjoyable nonetheless.
Anne Riesling: Much more restricted in quantity, and usually only released with 5 or 6 years bottle age. Very fine wine with its own unmistakeable apple-tang flavour. Has enormous cellaring potential but its character changes far less than (say) Lindemans whites as it ages.

Mt Pleasant Rhine Riesling Traminer: Released in recent years with some residual sugar (styled late-picked). A wine with a great deal of flavour, and certainly does not rely purely on the sugar to prop it up. Nice acid on finish helps the wine.

Philip Hermitage: After a run of fairly dismal wines, the currently available '75 Philip is a vast improvement. Good fruit, with a nice touch of spice on the bouquet and good length on the palate.

Mt Pleasant Cabernet Hermitage: Rich wines with Cabernet evident but the wines held in check by the aroma of tar.

Mt Pleasant Cabernet: A wine of real potential but held back for reasons similar to many of the wines.

Robert Hermitage: Some very good releases, usually with about 10 years bottle age, have been made in the past 3 or 4 years. Rich concentrated flavours and good balance.

Best buys: Anne Riesling 1974: $5.15

Philip Hermitage 1975: $4.65

Cellaring potential: Elizabeth Riesling 3–4 years; Anne Riesling 7–15 years; Philip Hermitage 5–10 years; Robert Hermitage 10+ years.

Cellar door sales/facilities: Open Monday to Saturday 9 am to 5 pm. Winery tours 10 am, 11 am and 12 noon. Full tasting facilities.

Retail distribution: National.

Summary: The Mount Pleasant label still has a devoted and loyal band of followers, but given the exceptional vineyards which McWilliams have, the wines — particularly the reds — should be much better than they are.

CB Marsh Estate

Formerly known as Quentin winery, the vineyard and winery were purchased late in 1978 by former pharmacist, Peter Marsh from Dr Quentin Taperell. Marsh, with a love of wine but little practical experience of winemaking, moved in on Christmas

Eve. With the innocence of the newborn, he and his family tackled the '79 vintage on their own. It was an experience which Peter Marsh acknowledges he will not quickly forget.

Nonetheless, his wines made the grade. A commendable '79 Pokolbin Riesling, a '78 Shiraz (made by Taperell but bottled by Marsh) and a '79 vintage Port are among the wines so far released. For a relatively small operation, the range of wines offered is extensive: a Traminer, Traminer Riesling, Moselle, and Cabernet complete a full offering of wine styles.

Established: 1971.

Address: Deasey Road, Pokolbin, 13 km north west of Cessnock. (049) 987 587.

Winemaker: Peter Marsh.

Annual crush: 65 tonnes.

Principal wines/wine styles

Pokolbin Semillon 1979: Clean, solid, old-style Semillon, with lots of character to bouquet. Very big, solid wine on palate in positive White-Burgundy mould. Will come on fairly quickly, and never be particularly elegant. Clean and well made, however.

Pokolbin Riesling 1979: Also made from Semillon, but early picked, fresher and with more lifted fruit flavour on bouquet. Much crisper fruit on palate and pleasant acid finish. An altogether pleasant wine.

Best buys

Pokolbin Semillon 1979: $2.95

Pokolbin Riesling 1979: $2.95

(Prices current May 1980)

Cellaring potential: Whites, 2–3 years; reds, 3–5 years.

Cellar door sales/facilities: Open Monday to Saturday 10 am to 4 pm; Sunday noon to 5 pm. Full tasting facilities.

Retail distribution: Restricted, Sydney (West Lindfield Cellars, Eastwood Cellars & Cammeray Cellars). Principal sales cellar door and mailing list. Inquiries welcome.

Summary: Clean, pleasantly flavoured wines with approach of new owner already evident in contrast between early picked and later picked Semillons. Marsh has already established his competence as a winemaker, and some good wines will undoubtedly come from this vineyard.

CB Maxwell's Maluna

The Maluna vineyard was one of the first planted in the Pokolbin district. On deep volcanic soil in a little-visited side valley, the vines grow with much vigour. Overcropping can be an occasional problem with such an unlikely variety as the usually shy-bearing Pinot Noir. The original vineyards went out of production in 1930, and were not re-established until 1971 when Sydney anaesthetist, Dr Don Maxwell, purchased the property.

Chardonnay, Pinot Noir, Semillon, Cabernet Sauvignon and Shiraz constitute the main plantings, all on virus-free clones. The wines are made for Dr Maxwell by Hungerford Hill, but he involves himself to a significant degree in the picking and winemaking decisions.

Established: 1971.

Address: Pokolbin Mountains Road, Pokolbin, 12 km west of Cessnock.

Winemakers: Dr D. C. Maxwell; Hungerford Hill Ltd.

Annual crush: 125 tonnes estate grown.

Principal wine/wine styles

Chardonnay: Some very good wines released although seldom available for any length of time. The '79 had considerable oak flavour but good fruit underneath. The '80 should be excellent.

Hermitage: Perhaps not the best variety to grow on the rich soils, sometimes tending to lack complexity and strength.

Pinot Noir: A very consistent, well-above-average line. Lovely raspberry fruit, quite fresh and delicate.

Cabernet Sauvignon: Some excellent clean Cabernets of good colour, flavour and structure; the '78 vintage is fairly light bodied, with gentle Cabernet character and perhaps just a little lactic on the bouquet.

Best buys: Chardonnay (when available). Cabernet Sauvignon 1978: $3.50

Cellaring potential: Hermitage and Pinot Noir, 2–3 years; Cabernet Sauvignon, 3– 4 years.

Cellar door sales/facilities: Open Monday to Saturday, 10 am to 5 pm; Sunday noon to 5 pm. Tasting facilities.

Retail distribution: Very limited. Cellar door/mail orders welcomed. Inquiries to PO Box 125, Woollahra, 2025.

Summary: An interesting mode of operation, with the fruit grown in one of the rare microclimatic situations on the fringe of the Hunter Valley which gives well-above-average yields.

Millstone Vineyard

The newest entrant in the Hunter Valley winestakes (at May 1980) and not surprisingly one of the smallest. A family-and-friends operation, in the words of owner — winemakers Peter and Vivienne Dobinson: "it has always been our intention to produce small quantities of distinctive, hand crafted wines . . ." Prices are high, but quantity is limited.

Established: 1973.

Address: Talga Road, Allandale, via Maitland, 2321. (049) 30 7317.

Winemaker: Peter Dobinson.

Annual sales: 255 dozen.

Principal wines/wine styles

First release in March 1980 was of the following parcels of wine: *Cabernet Sauvignon 1978*: 115 dozen. 2 years in small French and American oak casks.

Shiraz 1979: 85 dozen. 12 months in small American oak.

Sauvignon Blanc 1979: 55 dozen. 12 months in a French oak puncheon.

Best buys: Cabernet Sauvignon: $5.00

Shiraz 1979: $4.50
Sauvignon Blanc: $5.00
Cellar door sales/facilities: By appointment only.
Retail distribution: Not surprisingly, nil. All sales by mail order to above address.
Summary: Interesting varietal wines (Ruby Cabernet and Chardonnay yet to come from the 8 hectare vineyard) produced in miniscule quantities.

XX Mistletoe Farm

Mistletoe Farm was the name of an 80 acre property on which grapes were first planted in 1909. They flourished, but the vineyard went out of production in the depression years.

It was this block which formed the nucleus of the Hermitage Estate plantings in 1967, and the soil performed the same magic.

The Wyndham group has revived the name and created some of the most remarkable labels I have ever come across. The black and white reproductions do not do justice to the resplendent mock satin iridescent pink, green and purple finish of the originals. Wolf Blass, watch out!

At the time of writing, no wine was yet on sale but marketing should be under way by the time of publication.

XX Mount View

Harry and Anne Tulloch have been patiently getting Mount View together for some time now. Harry Tulloch has a reputation second to none as a vineyard manager based on a deep knowledge of clonal selection and an attention to the finest details of planting and layout techniques. His vineyards have a distinctly military air about them, so great is the precision of the

serried rows of healthy straight backed vines. The long delayed
opening of their vineyard tasting facilities — now scheduled for
about the time of publication of this book — has been due to the
dual constraints of building a winery and new home.

In Anne Tulloch's words: "We are making an attempt to
construct an old Australian homestead style of building and will
have a wine storage and tasting room incorporated. We feel we
should continue with the informal and friendly approach to
selling which Harry's family helped evolve in the early Hunter
days. The house and winery are in close proximity, so visitors
can choose to call in at whichever they find more interesting".

Established: 1970.
Address: Mount View Road, Mount View, 9 km south west of
Cessnock. (1049) 90 3307.
Winemaker: Harry Tulloch.
Annual crush: 14 tonnes.
Principal wines/wine styles
From 1974 to 1977 wines were made from Tulloch's grapes by
Drayton's Bellevue; Harry Tulloch's own winery was in opera-
tion for the 1980 vintage. Wines to be released when tasting
facilities open will be:
Hermitage: Vintages 1974, 1975 and 1977.
Cabernet Sauvignon: 1975.
Semillon Verdelho: 1977, 1970.
Prices were not determined at the time of writing.
Summary: One of the smallest wineries situated in the most
beautiful part of the Hunter Valley and determined to make the
visitor feel part of the family.

CB Oakdale Vineyards

"First planted 1866. Re-established 1970" — the letterhead tells much of the proud history of this vineyard, nestling on rolling foothills underneath the Brokenback range. Owned by a syndicate of about 19 members (principally lawyers) Oakdale has had something of a grim struggle because it does not have its own operating winery — if one ignores the old Audrey Wilkinson structure. From the '79 vintage, significant quantities of wine have been made for Oakdale at Drayton's Bellevue winery, allowing Oakdale to offer a much wider range of wine than the occasional offering of red wine in previous years.

Established: 1866.
Address: De Beyers Road, Pokolbin, 10 km west of Cessnock.
Winemaker: Drayton's Bellevue.

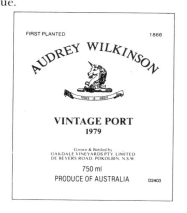

Principal wines/wine styles

Audrey Wilkinson Hunter River Riesling 1979: Clean and fresh, with the extra depth of fruit flavour that one expects from this vintage. Good balance and set for fairly early drinking.

Audrey Wilkinson Hermitage 1978: Another well made, clean wine. Medium colour, fresh fruity nose. Firm palate with quite perceptible tannin on the finish.

Audrey Wilkinson Vintage Port 1979: Made from late-picked Shiraz and fortified with fine brandy spirit.

Best buys: Hunter River Riesling 1979 (or 1980): $3.00
Hermitage 1978: $3.00
Vintage Port 1979: $4.00

Cellaring potential: Semillon 2–3 years; Hermitage 3–5 years. Port 5–10 years.

Cellar door sales/facilities: Open Saturdays and public holidays 10 am to 5 pm; Sundays noon to 5 pm. Full tasting facilities in old Audrey Wilkinson winery.

Retail distribution: Virtually nil. Sales cellar door and mail order. Inquiries welcome to GPO Box 314, Sydney, 2001.

Summary: A beautifully situated vineyard planted to some interesting varietals but yet to fully realize the potential of its re-establishment.

Penfolds Wines

Penfolds' presence in the Hunter Valley is little more than a token one compared with its heyday. First came the ill-fated decision in the early '60s to move from Dalwood at Branxton to Wybong in the Upper Hunter; then came the sale of Wybong to Rosemount Estates. Now all Penfolds Hunter whites (there are no reds) are made for them under contract at Wybong. The fruit, incidentally, comes principally from the old Hunter Valley Distillery vineyard in the Lower Hunter which Penfolds retained when they made their move up the Valley. The quality of the white wines (Bin 365 Pinot Riesling, Bin 700 HV Blanquette and 6K Semillon) is unremarkable.

Established: 1942.

Address: Hunter Valley District Vineyard, Pokolbin.

Principal wines/wine styles

Pinot Riesling Bin 365: The largest-selling wine made in the Hunter, and distributed throughout Australia. Seems to lack the flavour and structure it once had.

Hunter Valley Blanquette Bin 700: A relatively undistinguished wine made from an equally undistinguished variety.

Hunter Semillon Bin 6K: The first vintage (1973) in this line was a superb wine which won numerous gold medals. Follow-on versions have had nowhere near the quality, but are certainly acceptable wines.

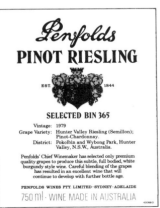

41

Best buys: Pinot Riesling Bin 365: $3.05
Hunter Semillon Bin 6K: $3.50
Cellaring potential: 3–5 years.
Retail distribution: Bin 365 national; others largely NSW.
Summary: The death throes of a once-great Hunter Valley operation are saddening to watch.

AA Robson Vineyard

Murray Robson is another of the remarkable individuals scattered throughout the wine industry of today. Elegance and style, overworked words though they are, encapsulate the Robson approach to wine and winemaking, from his impossibly neat, doll's-house winery to the roses at the end of the rows of vines to the classic simplicity of his label (the best in Australia, in my view).

The same qualities extend to the wines themselves — miraculously, because when in 1974 he made his first wines, he did not drink alcohol and had no palate whatsoever. He still drinks sparingly, but has learned a prodigious amount in the meantime. His red and white wines stand at the very forefront of the small wineries of Australia today. (If I had to limit my cellar to four small wineries they would be Balgownie, Robson, Petaluma and of course Brokenwood.)

His most publicised and consistent successes have been scored by a number of very good to great Chardonnays. The 1979 is at present showing a considerable degree of oak and I am not sure he was particularly lucky with the new casks he purchased for that year. However, he also makes excellent Semillon and a number of other varietal whites, the latter in very small quantities. In 1979 he also made 50 dozen of a fascinating sweet white, crammed full of complex flavour.

His immaculately produced reds are equally impressive. They have lovely colour, are utterly clean and have excellent balance. The range of 1979s are, in a word, great. There is a straight Cabernet, a rare Cabernet Merlot Hermitage, and a stunning Hermitage, which is at this stage the best of the three wines.

Established: 1972.
Address: Mount View Road, Mount View, 2325, 9 km southwest of Cessnock. (049) 903 670.
Winemaker: Murray Robson.
Annual sales: 9000 cases.
Principal wines/wine styles
Chardonnay: Lavish show success at national levels in the early years has firmly fixed this wine in the mind of the public and it

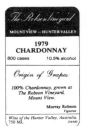

invariably sells out overnight. Whether it deserves such high standing compared with Robson's other wines is open to doubt, but it is quite clearly a great wine and well worth the effort involved to procure it. The fruit tends to be delicate early and the oak a little assertive, but come into balance with bottle age.

Semillon: Smoother and rounder than many others when young, always possessing a great deal of flavour. Usually have excellent colour into the bargain.

Hermitage: Robson has refined his winemaking to the point where sometimes one feels the wines are almost too perfect. There is no such feeling about the 1979 and yet it is as perfect a young wine as one could wish to see. Intense purple blue, lovely fruit bouquet perfectly balanced by oak, and a long complete palate. It has everything it should have and nothing it should not have.

Cabernet: Invariably crystal-clean wines these days, with intense purple colour and strong varietal bouquet. The wines are cleaned and polished in steel before being transferred to oak, a common enough procedure in large wineries but less so in small ones; it seems to subtly alter the character of the wine. Refinement, smoothness, crispness and excellent Cabernet flavour mark these wines.

Other varietals/varietal blends: Made in minute quantities and always worth pursuing.

Best buys
Hermitage 1979: $4.50
Chardonnay 1980: Not fixed at time of writing.
Cellaring potential: As the wines are relatively low in tannin, they will probably mature marginally more quickly than other comparable wines. Chardonnay, 3–6 years; Hermitage 3–5 years; Cabernet 4–6+ years.
Cellar door sales/facilities: Open Monday to Saturday 9 am to 5 pm; Sunday noon to 5 pm. Full tasting facilities, winery inspections welcome. Picturesque winery well worth a visit.
Retail distribution: Extremely limited. Sales cellar door and through mailing list. Well produced and comprehensive mailing list. Inquiries/orders welcome.

43

Summary: One of the great boutique wineries, producing first-class wines without regard to cost of production and never compromising on quality.

AA The Rothbury Estate

The graceful winery which houses Rothbury will be one of the landmarks of the Valley for generations to come; and the National Trust 100 years hence will no doubt have its plaque affixed by the front entrance.

Yet another product of the late '60s boom, Rothbury has also had to struggle to survive in the '70s. This struggle has never had the least root in the quality of its white wines, which are second to none in the period 1972–80. Rather, it reflected an excess of red-vine plantings and the burden of an interest bill on borrowed funds which far over-ran their planned duration.

Life is not yet easy, and Rothbury has a long way to go with its red wines, but its reputation as a maker of fine white wines is beyond challenge. These have an as yet untested life span. Ignoring the ill-fated '71 vintage (decimated by rain and mouldy fruit) the '72s are virtually as fresh as the day they were made, and the '73s have years of life left in them; with the odd exception, the same pattern continues through the younger vintages.

Rothbury has uncompromisingly placed its money on the proposition that Semillon will withstand all challenges as *the* white wine grape of the Hunter Valley. Its essays into varieties are unimportant. Rather, its magic stems from an enormously skilled selection of fruit from different blocks and of various maturation techniques (steel and oak) to provide an interesting and complex range of first-class Hunter whites.

Established: 1968.
Address: Broke Road, Pokolbin, 10 km north of Cessnock. (049) 987 555.
Winemaker: Murray Tyrrell (consultant).
Annual crush: 1800 tonnes.

Principal wines/wine styles

Vineyard Whites: Four Semillons are released each year from each of the four vineyards comprising the Rothbury group: Brokenback, Herlstone, Homestead Hill and Rothbury. It is these wines which have established Rothbury in the eyes of many as the top maker of white wines in the Valley today. They age magnificently, and when first released are of relative austerity. With 5 or more years age they are superb, although they tend to the more elegant style.

Individual Paddock White: Distinguished by its black label, only one Individual Paddock White is made each year and is the top wine. Even then the quantity will be strictly dependent on the quality of the available base-material and is usually very restricted. Great wines.

Varietal Whites: A number of varietal whites (Semillon, Chardonnay, Traminer, Traminer Riesling and the like) are made in small quantities. They have done little to upset the Rothbury philosophy that Semillon is the classic Hunter white variety, but are always eagerly sought and sell out quickly.

Wood Matured White: A wood-matured Semillon is made each year for release under the black label. An extremely complex wine of considerable interest and quality which demands cellaring.

Vineyard Reds: Correspond in labelling to the vineyard whites. So far at least, they are not of the same outstanding quality. Soft, pleasant and fairly early maturing styles have been the norm to date.

Individual Paddock Red: The 73 "Bin A" was a marvellous wine, and there have been one or two others along the way which have impressed greatly.

Best buys

1980 Vintage Vineyard Whites: $3.25
1979 Wood Matured White: $4.25 (approx)
(Prices cellar door to members, current through 1980)

Cellaring potential: Semillons: 3 to 10+ years. (The '72 Rothbury Estate White clearly has years left in it. Lindemans whites benefit from 15 or more years in bottle; there is no reason why Rothbury should not do the same.)
Vineyard Reds: 3 to 5+ years.

Cellar door sales/facilities: Open 9 am to 5 pm Monday to Saturday; noon to 5 pm Sunday. Very fine facilities in a spectacular winery complex.

Retail distribution: Until recently extremely restricted, but now increasing in NSW. Most sales through membership of the Rothbury Estate Society which is open to all. Inquiries welcome; simply write to the Estate.

Summary: Membership of the Rothbury Estate is a must for anyone with the least love of Hunter Semillons. The range of fringe benefits is very nearly (but not quite) as impressive as the range of wines available.

BB Saxonvale

Only Rosemount could shade Saxonvale in growth since 1976 and none in terms of complexities of growth. Saxonvale now covers four distinct vineyards, three sales outlets and spreads from Pokolbin to Mt Leonard and thence to Fordwich.

Like Rosemount, the 1979 vintage whites suggest the rapid increase in quantity has placed strains on quality. The Chardonnays were exceptionally fine flagships to a fine fleet of wines in both 1977 and 1978. The 1979 standard Pinot Chardonnay did not have the same quality, nor did a number of other wines from that vintage. The '79 Bin Chardonnay, a later release, was a welcome return to form.

Looked at on overall performance to date, Saxonvale produces top class Chardonnay; good, rich and fairly quick-maturing Semillons; clean fruity reds with above-average colour and well-handled oak flavour to complement the fresh fruit flavour. The whites basically come from the Fordwich vineyards; the reds from the Pokolbin Estates and Happy Valley vineyards.

Established: 1971.

Address: Happy Valley Vineyard, Oakey Creek Road, Pokolbin; Pokolbin Estates vineyard and tasting room McDonalds Road, Pokolbin; Fordwich Estate, Broke 2330. Phone: (0657921) 39.

Winemaker: Mark Cashmore.

Annual crush: 4000 tonnes.

Principal wines/wine styles

20 different white table wines, 6 reds, 2 roses, 2 sparkling wines and 1 port give a fair indication of the product emphasis at Saxonvale. The best of the wines are usually:

Chardonnay Bin 1: At the top of its form one of the very best Chardonnays made in the country. Gains power and complexity continuously throughout its first 3 or 4 years in bottle and richly repays those who are patient. Oak and fruit are very skilfully balanced against each other. The 1979 vintage has excellent balance, good acid and should develop very well.

Limited Release White Burgundy: A full-bodied Semillon given some time in oak, rich and textured.

Semillon: Always slightly fuller in structure than Lower Hunter versions and certainly much fuller than Upper Hunter.

(Fordwich is halfway, geographically, between the two). Develops reasonably quickly into golden, honeyed style.

Cabernet Sauvignon: Good colour, clean fruit–oak bouquet and fresh crisp palate with varietal flavour evident but not overwhelming. A very good, in-between style which does not require extensive cellaring.

Best buys: Chardonnay 1979 Bin 1: $3.95 (approx.)
Cabernet Sauvignon 1977: $3.30

Cellaring potential: Semillon 2–5 years; Chardonnay 3–6+ years; Cabernet Sauvignon 3–5 years.

Cellar door sales/facilities: Open 8.30 am to 5 pm Monday to Saturday; Sunday, noon to 5 pm. 3 locations headed by 2 Pokolbin outlets give ample access to wines. Old stone cottage at Pokolbin Estates very picturesque.

Retail distribution: Extensive throughout NSW and increasing in Melbourne.

Summary: Against the run of play, a major success story over the difficult years 1976–80. Produces a range of impressive whites headed by Chardonnay and good reds.

B Tamburlaine Wines

Dr Lance Allen followed closely in the footsteps of fellow medical practitioner Max Lake, and still remembers the days when his vineyard was one of only three small winemaker operations offering wines to the public — Lake's Folly and Belbourie being the other two. There are now five times that number and it is easy to get lost in the crowd.

Dr Allen takes time off from his busy Cessnock medical practice to make the wine; his wife and children look after the sales desk and assist in running the winery and packaging the wine. Their personal touch and involvement is evident at all points of production down to special releases celebrating the birth of grandchildren and the like. The marketing of the wine is extremely low key: Mrs Allen candidly says: "Lance is only interested in making the wine and looking after the vines. He leaves the selling to me". There is always a friendly reception for visitors to the unpretentious winery; the wines are a bonus.

Established: 1966.

Address: McDonalds Road, Pokolbin. (049) 987 570.

Winemaker: Dr Lance Allen.

Annual crush: 35 tonnes.

Annual sales: 1500 cases.

Principal wines/wine styles

Pokolbin Semillon 1979: Yet another first class white wine from this outstanding vintage. Excellent bouquet: clean and fruity. Good balance to palate which shows traditional Hunter Semillon flavour. Great cellaring prospect.

Pokolbin Semillon (oak matured) 1979: Very similar wine with oak flavour kept well in restraint. A very good wine indeed; it will also develop excellently in bottle.

Pokolbin Dry Red Vat 9, 1977: Gold medal winner at 1978 Hunter Valley Wine Show. Only 240 dozen made. Matured in small Nevers oak casks, and shows all of the concentrated flavour of this drought year. Strong tannin and oak match the heavy fruit. A wine with a very long future.

Cabernet Shiraz 1977: Again matured in Nevers oak, but a little lighter in body and flavour. Will be ready sooner, but is at present a little hard on the finish.

Cabernet Sauvignon 1978: Made from grapes purchased from the Upper Hunter. Light style, but with pronounced varietal flavour. Well made wine.

Cellaring potential: Semillon 3 to 5 years, but nonetheless offering very good drinking now. Reds 4 to 6 years.

Best buys: Pokolbin Semillon 1979: $3.00

Pokolbin Semillon (oak) 1979: $3.00

Pokolbin Dry Red Vat 9 1977: $3.50

Prices cellar door (by the dozen) current May 1980.

Cellar door sales/facilities: Open Monday to Saturday 10 am to 4 pm. Tasting facilities. Cellar door sales welcome.

Retail distribution: John Urwick Cellars, Sydney sole retail outlet. Mail orders welcome to PO Box 28, Cessnock, 2325.

Summary: Low yielding vineyard produces full flavoured reds and some first class whites. All wines are made in very small quantities and equal amounts of white and red will be made in future.

Terrace Vale

Terrace Vale, founded by a syndicate of friends in 1971, has been producing its own wine since 1975. In that relatively short period it has established itself as one of the finest, if not the finest, small white-wine maker.

Its whites do undoubtedly shade its reds. The latter are sound, well-made wines but they lack complexity, and thereby, final quality. It may have something to do with the soil on which they are grown; I do not know.

The whites are an altogether different proposition. The Semillons develop a marvellous depth of honeyed (not sweet) flavour while still fairly young, but without the faintest hint of coarseness. At two to three years of age they have few equals. Time alone will show how long they will live, but I am not sure it really matters.

I believe the '79 Chardonnay Bin 2 was the best released in the Hunter Valley out of the '79 vintage. I had supported the wine since the day it was released but it had one or two eminent detractors. One of those was present at a blind tasting of over 20 Chardonnays from the '79 vintage judged under strict show conditions; I was delighted when he (and I) were among the overwhelming majority who placed what turned out to be the Terrace Vale as their top wine.

The '79 has long since sold out, but the '80 vintage should be available around the time of publication. I should not waste time trying to taste it before ordering: you will probably miss out.

Established: 1971.

Address: Deasey Lane, Pokolbin, 2321, 15 km north of Cessnock. (049) 987517.

Winemaker: Alain le Prince.

Annual crush: 130 tonnes.

Principal wines/wine styles

Semillon Bin 1 and Bin 1A: Bin 1A is always the bigger wine of the two and usually the better. Bin 1 is fresh, delicate and fruity but has character from a relatively early stage. Bin 1A is noted for its glorious green-gold colour and the depth and breadth of fruit flavour which builds quickly.

Traminer Bin 3: Very distinct, quite broad varietal flavour filled out even further by a small amount of residual sugar. In no way sweet but definitely adds to overall flavour levels. A big, early drinking style.

Chardonnay Bin 2: Gloriously flavoured wines, green-gold in colour and with tremendous depth of fruit—oak flavour. Extremely rich and texured, more in Californian style than Australian. Trace of residual sugar adds to richness of wine and in no way obtrudes on varietal flavour.

Shiraz Bin 6 and Bin 6A: Bin 6 has much less oak than Bin 6A. Clean, well-made wines but not, so far at least, particularly exciting. The '79 vintage may well turn the tide, and is, I understand, a superb young red.

Cabernet Shiraz: A particularly fine '79 is in the pipeline at the time of writing.

Cabernet Sauvignon: Not previously released, but a very good '79 will be on sale by the time of publication.

Best buys (approx. prices): 1980 Semillon Bin 1: $4.00

1980 Chardonnay Bin 2: $5.00

1979 Cabernet Shiraz: $4.00

Cellaring potential: Semillon 2–4+ years; Chardonnay 2–5+ years; reds 3–6 years.

Cellar door sales/facilities: Open 10 am to 4 pm Saturday; noon to 4 pm Sunday. Tasting facilities.

Retail distribution: Limited through the Stone Wine Company. Main sales through well organized mailing list. Inquiries welcome to GPO Box 14, Sydney.

Summary: An outstanding maker of intensely flavoured and structured Semillons and Chardonnay, and full-flavoured Traminer. Reds on the way up.

◣ Tullochs

The ownership of Tullochs has changed three times in the past ten years (from Tulloch family to Reed International to Gilbeys) but the vineyard management and winemaking practices have mercifully been left undisturbed other than for the injection of considerable capital for winery buildings and equipment.

The winery is situated in the heart of Pokolbin, but much of the fruit comes from Tulloch's Fordwich vineyards. This results in whites and reds which stand a little apart from most lower Hunter wines, but are none the worse for that.

Indeed, both white and red wines are of first quality. The Private Bin Semillon (called Riesling, of course), the Semillon Verdelho and Semillon Chardonnay are beautiful wines which benefit enormously from bottle age. The '74 Semillon Chardonnay was outstanding but subsequent vintages have been excellent too, with '77 (still available at the time of writing) particularly fine. The whites tend to have more backbone than – and perhaps not the flexibility nor final development potential of – conventional Lower Hunter Semillons, but are very good wines withal.

The red wines are old favourites of mine, and even more than the whites reflect the microclimate of the Fordwich district. They are supple, complex wines of medium body which age very well. Some excellent Hermitage was made in both '75 and '76 and is currently available. Even greater Cabernets were made, and these are yet to be released.

Established: 1893.

Address: De Beyers Road, Pokolbin 2321, 10 km north-west of Cessnock, (049) 987 503.

Winemaker: Patrick Auld.

Annual crush & Sales: Not disclosed.

Principal wines/wine styles

Hunter River Riesling: Tullochs stick to the old-style nomenclature for Semillon. Two releases are made each year, the standard, about six months after vintage, and the private bin a year or so after that. Not only because of the extra bottle age, but also because of the extra fruit complexity, the private bin is certainly worth the extra money. Some magnificent wines have been released under this label, none better than the '74 which is still winning gold medals virtually at will. The style is on the elegant side, almost austere, but always very good.

Semillon Chardonnay: A blend started in the early '70s and one of the very best made in the Hunter. The '74 was again outstanding, while the '77 (still available at the time of writing) was very nearly as good. Complex fruit flavours complemented by some oak are balanced by a very firm, crisp finish which augurs well for further bottle age.

Semillon Verdelho: An unusual blend, the quality of which is very close to that of the Semillon Chardonnay. A rich, velvety, long-lived wine.

Private Bin Dry Red: Ever reliable, ever enjoyable wines usually released with 5 or more years bottle age and therefore more or less ready, although most will continue to hold and marginally improve for many years. Made from Hermitage, principally Fordwich grown but with some Pokolbin material.

White Label Hermitage: Special bottling of smaller parcels of wine of outstanding quality released under this label from time to time. The '73 and '76 vintages (the latter just released) were outstanding, with complexity and good colour.

White Label Cabernet Sauvignon: Again some quite exceptional releases. The Cabernet character is softer than some, but clearly defined all the same. The wines' main strength lies in their superb balance.

Best buys
1979 Private Bin Hunter Riesling: $4.55
1978 Semillon Chardonnay: $4.68

1976 White Label Hermitage: $5.15
Cellaring potential: Whites 3−7+ years; reds 5−9+ years.
Cellar door sales/facilities: Open 9 am to 4.45 pm Monday to Thursday; 9 am to 4.15 pm Friday and Saturday; noon to 5 pm Sunday. Full tasting facilities and winery inspections welcome.
Retail distribution: National.
Summary: Tullochs is one of the most reliable of all Hunter vineyards, producing reds which possibly cage out their whites but both of which offer remarkable consistency of style and quality from one vintage to the next.

Tyrrells

The Tyrrell family has owned and managed this vineyard since it was founded in 1858. Its moderate size and traditional winemaking methods (open concrete fermentation tanks and earthen floors) belie its role as one of the foremost wineries in New South Wales.

Tyrrells' Chardonnay is the most eagerly sought white wine made in the Hunter, and together with a series of absolutely first-class Semillons, leaves no room for argument about the quality of its whites. These benefit enormously from extended bottle age. Over the past few vintages, new-style early-drinking varietals have also appeared, with a Sauvignon Blanc finding enormous market appeal.

Its Hermitage-based reds have always been clean, sturdy but at times straightforward. Recently Pinot Noir, Cabernet and Cabernet Hermitage blends have widened the range and offered greater complexity.

Both reds and whites have been prolific show award winners, and the Chardonnay and Pinot Noir have had spectacular success in competitions against French and Californian wines.
Established: 1858.
Address: Broke Road, Pokolbin, 12 km north-west of Cessnock. (049) 987509.
Winemakers: Ralph Fowler, Murray Tyrrell.
Annual crush: 860 tonnes, principally estate grown.
Principal wine/wine styles
Vats 1, 15 and 18 Riesling: Usually Vat 1 is the top Semillon of the vintage, but not always. Impeccable winemaking and quality control coupled with fruit from some of the best white grape — Semillon, of course — vineyards in the Hunter ensure wines of the utmost quality. Because they are made in relatively small quantities, there is vintage variation, but it is more in style than in quality.

Vat 47 Chardonnay: Murray Tyrrell pioneered Chardonnay in the Hunter and undoubtedly understands more about it than any other maker. Every year it disputes overall top billing with Vat 1, but for the wine-buying public there is no contest. Marvellous combination of ripe fruit with French oak gives great complexity; if any one doubts the staying power of the wine they should find someone with a bottle of the '73, which is quite superb now.

Vat 16 Blanquette; Vat 3 Blanquette Shiraz: Only Tyrrells handle these wines with such flair, and occasionally they produce the top wines of the vintage (Vat 3 in 1970; Vat 16 in 1975). The straight Blanquette is now made with some residual sugar and is extremely popular.

Vat 63 Pinot Riesling (Chardonnay – Semillon by any other name): Always close to the top, and often drinks very well from an early age – say 2 years.

Varietals: A full range of varietals and varietal blends (Sauvignon Blanc, Traminer and Traminer Riesling) are released and are some of the best made in the Lower or Upper Hunter.

Vats 5, 8, 9 and 11 Winemaker's Selection Dry Reds: Almost invariably these four vats – coming each year from the same vineyards — are picked by Tyrrells as their top wines. More subtle use of oak and the use of small quantities of Cabernet when the vintage demands it, has resulted in greater complexity than in earlier vintages (pre 1973). Since that year these wines have been consistent trophy and gold medal winners, storming even the bastion of the Adelaide Show to take the Montgomery Trophy outside South Australia for the first time. ('75 Vat 11 at the '78 Adelaide Show).

Pinot Noir: Tyrrells Pinot Noir recently was awarded the highest points of 300 wines from all over the world at the Gault Millaut Wine Olympics in Paris, and was selected by the organizers as one of the 12 great wines of the world along with Petrus, Mouton Rothschild and the like. Regrettably, it is not that good, but the line is clearly the most interesting of its type coming out of Australia today. The '79 vintage is outstanding.

Best buys

Vat 18 Riesling 1980: $3.75
Vat 1 Riesling 1980: $4.20
Vat 47 Chardonnay 1980: $5.00
Vat 9 Dry Red: $4.00
Vat 70 Cabernet Sauvignon: $3.35
(Prices cellar door — current through 1980).

Cellaring potential: Semillon (Rieslings) 2–7+ years; Chardonnay 3–7+ years; Hermitage 4–6 years; Cabernet 4–8+ years.

Cellar door sales/facilities: Open Monday to Saturday 8 am to 5 pm. Tasting facilities; winery inspections; BBQ and picnic facilities in immaculately maintained grounds.

Retail distribution: All the top Vat (or private bin) wines are pre-sold on mail order and at cellar door. Retail distribution (extensive NSW) is of generic styles which represent very good value for money.

Summary: A once medium-sized winery which has made the transition to the big league and yet managed to maintain its very high standards. Superb white wines and good reds.

C Wollundry

Ron and Kay Hansen are another couple who decided to forsake the rat-race for a more leisurely life, although the decision to use part of their farm for growing grapes and making wine was something of an afterthought. A vintage working with Max Lake quite clearly taught Ron Hansen a good deal. Although the wines are seldom seen, even in Sydney, some are particularly good.

The white wines are distinctly full-bodied, made in the old style with the deliberate return of some of the pressings to the free run juice. They are solid, mouth filling wines, and what they lack in delicacy they certainly make up in flavour.

The reds are something of a contrast: very well-balanced and clean, they have a distinct elegance. Unlike his mentor, Hansen does not rely on new oak, and is content to let the natural grape flavour speak for itself.

Established: 1971.
Address: Palmers Lane, Pokolbin, 2321, 12 km north of Cessnock. (049) 987 572.
Winemaker: Ron Hansen.

Annual crush: 100 tonnes.
Principal wines/wine styles
3 or 4 dry reds, and an equal number of dry whites are usually available.
Blanquette "Oyster Wine" 1979: Strong Blanquette varietal character. A well named wine: dry and with a sharp tang, entirely suited to shellfish. Very reminiscent of some McWilliams/Draytons whites.
Semillon 1977: Big old-style wine; bouquet closed but clean. Heavy wine on the palate with lots of body and character.
Hermitage 1976: Colour of light to medium depth but of good hue. Attractive spicy Hermitage bouquet. Good structure and balance to a classic medium weight Hunter Hermitage.
Hermitage Cabernet 1978: Clean, light wine with hint of "friars balsam" on nose. Nice balance, easy drinking.

Best buys
Semillon 1977: $3.20
Hermitage 1976: $2.95
Cellaring potential
White wines 3–5 years; reds 4–7 years.
Cellar door sales/facilities: Open Monday to Saturday 9 am to 5 pm; Sunday noon to 5 pm. Tasting and BBQ facilities.
Retail distribution: Very limited. Sunnybrook Wine Cellars, 4 Bridge St, Sydney. Cellar door sales/mail orders are chief outlets. Inquiries welcome.
Summary: Seldom encountered wines, even in Sydney, but very well worth the search (or the drive up the dirt road to the winery).

BA Wyndham Estate

Wyndham Estate is the oldest established vineyard still operating in Australia. What is more, it has been in continuous production since it was established in 1828. The vineyards have been totally replanted on several occasions, most recently between 1970 and 1972. Many of the historic buildings remain and provide one of the show pieces of the Hunter Valley.

Wyndham these days is the chief producing arm of a complex group of winemaking and marketing companies all ultimately owned by Australian Guarantee Corporation and Anglo Thai Corporation with 44% each and by Brian McGuigan with 12%. The immense financial strength of AGC and Anglo Thai fits synergistically with the marketing and promotional strength of the extraordinarily active Brian McGuigan. The sort of growth rate which the group has enjoyed is encapsulated in Black Label Traminer Riesling. First marketed in 1972, 2250 litres were made; in 1979 output was 720,000 litres.

The producing vineyards in the Wyndham Group (each of which is dealt with separately in this book) are Wyndham itself; Richmond Grove; Hollydene; Hermitage Estate and Elliott's Wines.

Wyndham produces a comprehensive range of white and red table wines released under both varietal and generic labels and covering the full gamut of the price range from $1.80 to $16.00. It is hard to keep up with the full extent of the range, and very easy to forget that in blind tastings its wines often outclass far more prestigous rivals. But reflecting on all of the numerous wines released by Wyndham which I have tasted over the last 6 months, the quite remarkable wines have to be the reds. Wyndham have learnt something which other makers have not about colour retention in Hunter reds, particularly given that much of the material used must be irrigated. Much the same comment applies to fruit flavour, the depth of which harks back to the Wyndham Bukkulla wines of the last century. Atypical Hunter wines by the standards of today: what they lose in elegance they make up in total flavour.

Established: 1828.
Address: Dalwood via Branxton, 2335. (049) 381311.
Winemaker: Brian McGuigan.
Annual sales: 270,000 cases.
Principal wines/wine styles
Chablis Superior: Made with remarkably consistent style and quality each year and one of the relatively few totally dry wines in the Wyndham stable. The '79 was highly regarded, but I had a few reservations about the fairly hard finish of what was essentially a very light bodied wine.
Gewurtz Traminer: (So-called by Wyndham, but Traminer by any other name.) Made with considerable residual sugar, it has

immense floral flavour on bouquet and palate. The sort of wine the purists sneer at and the average wine drinker consumes with absolute abandon.

Traminer Riesling: The flagship, and one which has retained remarkable flavour and quality given the tanker-load fulls in which it is produced. An object lesson in quality control to most of Wyndham's direct competitors. Nicely balanced fruit flavours and residual sugar make for a totally uncomplicated yet flavoursome wine.

Hunter River Riesling: Wood matured wines which are held back for several years prior to their release. Both the '77 and '78 wines (the latter released in May 1980) offered exceptional value for money, with a high-class marriage of fruit and oak with an unusual (for Semillon, that is, though not for Wyndham) trace of sweetness.

Cabernet Shiraz: The '76 is an extraordinary wine. At 4 years of age it gives the impression of a 4-day old wine — deep purple-blue colour, almost opaque; rich extractive berry flavour; and a trace of sweetness on the finish as if the fermentation was not quite complete. What all this has to do with the Hunter Valley, I am not quite sure, but it should certainly win a lot of admirers in the market place.

Trophy Cabernet Sauvignon '78: (With 2 trophies and 4 gold medals under its belt.) Exceptional colour, high alcohol nose suggesting very ripe fruit. Considerable varietal character balanced by American oak flavour and heavy tannic finish. A very big wine with a very long future (if the acid is there to sustain it).

Very Late Picked Riesling (Beerenauslese) '78: A nearly unique wine of a style which has not been seen from the Hunter in decades and may not be seen again for almost as long. There is no question botrytis did affect very markedly the grapes from which this wine was made. I saw it immediately after vintage when it was far from attractive, but all the ingredients were there. It is now golden orange, with an intense raisined character of great complexity — of its style, a great Australian wine. The only query is its forward development. (And its price — $16.00 a bottle.)

Best buys
Hunter River Riesling: $2.95
Traminer Riesling: $3.15
Cabernet Shiraz: $3.15

Cellaring potential: Aromatic white varietals drink now; Hunter River Riesling 2–3 years; Cabernet Shiraz and Cabernet 4–6+ years.

Cellar door sales/facilities: Comprehensive tasting and restaurant facilities in historic setting worth a visit for its own sake. Open Monday to Saturday 8 am to 6 pm; Sunday noon to 5 pm.

Retail distribution: Extensive through Taylor Ferguson/ Hunter Valley Wine Company.

Summary: Wyndham Estate is unabashed in producing and marketing commercially popular wine styles, which paradoxically tend to obscure the fact that it makes some wines of outstanding character and quality.

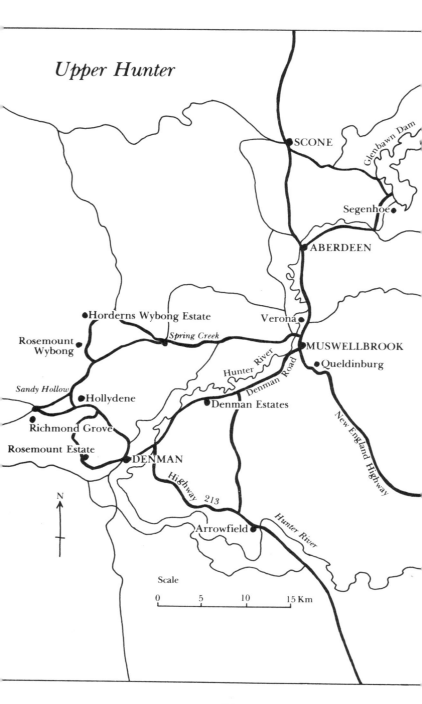

Upper Hunter

Glenbawn Dam

SCONE

Segenhoe

ABERDEEN

Horderns Wybong Estate

Verona

Rosemount Wybong

Spring Creek

MUSWELLBROOK

Queldinburg

Hunter River

Denman Road

Sandy Hollow

Hollydene

Denman Estates

Richmond Grove

New England Highway

Rosemount Estate

DENMAN

Highway 213

N

Arrowfield

Hunter River

Scale

0   5   10   15 Km

Upper Hunter Valley

The typical Upper Hunter vineyard is more than 100 hectares — often much larger — and is almost invariably irrigated. The much more numerous Lower Hunter vineyards are as small as five hectares and irrigation is not common. Just as red and white production is in almost exact balance in the Hunter as a whole, so is that between irrigated and non-irrigated vines; in the 1979 vintage 11,533 tonnes came from the former and 11,881 tonnes from the latter. Although figures separating Lower and Upper Hunter production are not available, this strongly suggests that output between the two districts is roughly comparable.

Another significant difference is the style of the wines. The Upper Hunter is the principal home of the aromatic white varietals, headed by Rhine Riesling, Traminer and Sauvignon Blanc. Chardonnay, too, is springing up at a similar rate here as in the Pokolbin district, and the Richmond Grove and Saxonvale wines of this variety can be as good as virtually any the Lower Hunter can produce.

All of these wines perform very well under high-yield conditions. I have no doubt that Rhine Riesling and Traminer in particular tend to become overblown and coarse in the Lower Hunter and that the ameliorating effects of climate and irrigation in the Upper Hunter are beneficial.

Such wines need relatively little time in the bottle and do not age gracefully. I recently saw a three-year-old Traminer, covered in show awards in its youth, which had entirely cracked up. This is no criticism: fresh, fruity and aromatic whites have as permanent and important a place in wine consumption as old White Burgundy styles. They simply serve different needs, and the young wines not infrequently have distinct price advantages.

I have been accused in the past of having a bias against irrigated wines. If I have a bias, it is against Hermitage stretched to yield six tonnes to the acre and more. At least with the red wine market as it is today, there is little place for such wines. Cabernet is a far better proposition, and some very pleasant reds from this variety come from the district.

The Wyndham group of companies (I include Hollydene and Hermitage) have produced a number of remarkably full-bodied and flavoursome reds, all presumably from irrigated material. Small quantities of specially handled show wines from other Upper Hunter wineries (Mt Dangar vineyards, in particular) have had exceptional colour and flavour, so it is clearly not impossible to make very good reds. It is simply that under normal commercial conditions the quality tends to range between adequate at best, and thin, brown and lacking at worst.

Scenically the district is enormously attractive, particularly in the growing season when luxuriantly clothed vines stretch as far as the eye can see. The wineries, too, are spectacular: large and modern, they feature all the sophisticated machinery and gadgetry which is essential to modern winemaking.

Arrowfield

Arrowfield underwent major surgery in 1979 in an attempt to transform itself from frog to prince. With 485 hectares of high-yielding, drip-irrigated vines and an annual crush of 4000 tonnes of grapes, it was the largest single vineyard operation in the Hunter. While the quantity of the output may have been impressive, the quality was not. Stocks accumulated on winery floor and retailers shelves, with the reds in particular being impossible to sell or — so it seemed — give away.

Part of the problem lay in red grape quality (poor) and part in the marketing philosophy that all wine produced on the estate should be sold under the Arrowfield name. Discounts do not compensate for lack of quality, and the strategy failed.

Red-wine production has now been slashed, and the emphasis placed on far smaller parcels of vintage varietals selling in the $2.95 to $3.25 range. Lesser wines are disposed of in bulk. The '79 whites demonstrate the real benefit of this policy in A38 Traminer Riesling, A42 Traminer and A59 Rhine Riesling — all fine wines, clean and with good varietal definition.

I see no reason why new winemaker Garry Baldwin (who produced the '79 vintage) should not continue to produce wines of similar if not better quality in future years.

Established: 1969.

Address: Highway 213, Jerry's Plains, 2330, 20 km south-east of Denman. (065) 76 4041.

Winemaker(s): Garry Baldwin; Assistants David Wollan, Adrian Sheridan.

Annual crush: 2000 tonnes.

Principal wines/wine styles

Seven varietal wines are produced from the seven varieties planted together with a Traminer Riesling blend.

Traminer: Deliberately made in a light and delicate style to avoid oiliness and bitterness associated with some of the bigger versions of this style. 1979 vintage was a very good, soft, light wine.

Rhine Riesling: Also tends towards lightness and benefits from 1 to 2 years bottle age.

Chardonnay: Maturation in new oak fills out a good wine, with the '79 vintage being particularly impressive but all released under other purchasers' labels.

Semillon: Typically, less rich and honeyed than Lower Hunter wines. Both oak and stainless steel releases.

Blanquette: Typical heavy fruit tending towards White Burgundy style. Not everyone's cup of tea.

Cabernet Sauvignon: The '76 vintage on offer has considerable maturity, showing some varietal character touched up by oak.

ARROWFIELD	**ARROWFIELD**
TRAMINER	**CHARDONNAY**
HUNTER VALLEY VINTAGE VARIETAL	HUNTER VALLEY VINTAGE VARIETAL
Bin A42	*Bin A7*
1979	*1978*
Arrowfield Wines. A Division of W. R. Carpenter Australia Ltd.	Arrowfield Wines. A Division of W. R. Carpenter Australia Ltd.
Early picking has produced a light, well balanced wine with a crisp acid finish. Chosen by Winestate Magazine as one of the best Traminers produced in 1979.	A wine with excellent straw-gold colour, being the result of maturation in wood. Its palate is a complex mixture of young Chardonnay and American Oak.
750ml	750ml
Produce of Australia	Produce of Australia
D4225	D4225

Shiraz: Along with Cabernet, will ultimately disappear from the Arrowfield range. The currently available 75 Bin A14 Shiraz is in fact a very pleasant, fairly light old wine.

Best buys
Rhine Riesling Bin A59 1979: $2.90.
Shiraz Bin A14 1975: $2.90.

Cellaring potential: White varietals (other than Chardonnay) 1–2 years, reds ready now.

Cellar door sales/facilities: Open 8 am to 4 pm Monday to Friday; 10 am to 4 pm Saturday. Striking winery complex; tours by appointment. Full tasting and B.B.Q. facilities.

Retail distribution: National, but emphasis now on New South Wales.

Summary: A recent transformation of winemaking and marketing practices has resulted in well-made, clear-flavoured varietal whites at reasonable prices and limited quantities of mature reds.

BC Denman Estate

The corporate history of Denman Estate has been painful. It was totally re-organised for the '79 vintage, with both vineyard and winemaking arrangements changing radically.

Until 1979, most of the wine was sold in bulk, and the small quantity available for cellar door sales was not worth the trip. Then Oenotech Pty Ltd (a wine consulting firm run by Messrs. Croser and Jordan) were put in charge of the vintage, and a whole series of excellent white wines — not to mention a few small parcels of red — resulted. In 1980, Ian Scarborough (ex Tullochs) took over the reins, and should ensure a continuation of the renaissance.

Most appear to be headed for early drinking, though all are clean, well-flavoured wines with clearly defined varietal character. The exercise proved conclusively just how greatly many of the new vineyards and wineries of the Upper Hunter in particular suffered from poor management and, in particular, poor winemaking skills in previous years.

Established: 1969.

Address: Denman Road, Muswellbrook, 2333. (065) 472 473.

Winemaker: Ian Scarborough (Scarmac Pty Ltd).

Annual Crush: 1200 tonnes.

Principal wines/wine styles

Rhine Riesling: Rich, almost voluptuous, varietal flavour tending towards tropical fruit style rather than the more steely type. Depth of flavour masks the acid, making for a soft, easy-drinking wine. Little difference in style between standard and private bin 39. Extremely well-made wines.

Traminer Riesling: Whenever good winemaking is applied this is a very acceptable, easy-drinking blend. The Traminer is quite pronounced but delicate.

Semillon/Hunter River Riesling: Again 2 releases, with confusion multiplied by the fact that both are from the same grape and both are similar in style and structure. The Semillon Bin 3 is a little fuller and firmer, but both show excellent varietal flavour and tend more to a Lower Hunter style. Very good.

White Burgundy: Yet another Semillon variant, slightly fuller in style and again excellent drinking.

Sauvignon Blanc: Clean and soft.

Traminer: Again 2 versions, standard and private bin, showing good varietal definition but sometimes a trace of the bitter—hard finish which dogs this variety.

Best buys

Rhine Riesling 1979: $2.75
Rhine Riesling Bin 39 1979: $3.15
White Burgundy 1979: $2.75
Semillon Bin 3 1979: $3.20

Cellaring potential: 1−3 years.

Cellar door sales/facilities: Open Monday to Friday 8 am to 4 pm.

Retail distribution: Available both wholesale and retail. Orders–inquiries to Bay House, 2 Guilfoyle Avenue (PO Box 138), Double Bay, 2028. Distribution so far restricted.

Summary: The quality of the wines was literally revolutionized in 1979, and the 1980 vintage should also be worth following.

BC Hollydene

Hollydene's radically designed yet highly functional winery-in-the-round is one of the landmarks of the Upper Hunter. The battery of Potter fermenters stand in a circle under the honeycomb roof, and are the nerve centre for the Upper Hunter production of the Wyndham Estate. The fairly modest sales of Hollydene wines give no indication of the importance of the winery to the group structure.

Winemaker Barry Platt was trained at Geigenheim, Germany, and clearly has an exceptional touch in the handling of white varietals. It was Platt's German schooling which led to his 1978 recognition of the botrytis infected fruit and his making of the remarkable Beerenauslese of that year — released under the Wyndham label. His handling of conventional wines — Semillon, Chardonnay and Rhine Riesling — is no less deft, and brings out the maximum possible flavour in all varieties. Unlike Richmond Grove, both red and white table wines are made.

Established: 1967.

Address: Merriwa Road, Hollydene, via Denman 10 km north west of township. (065) 472 316.

Winemaker: Barry Platt.

Annual crush: 2500 tonnes (for group).

Annual sales: 7500 cases.

Principal wines/wine styles

Hunter Valley Riesling: Both the '78 and '79 vintages of this wine showed similar structure and character and it is a fair bet the '80 will continue the line. The '79 (a trophy winner) has abundant rich semillon flavour augmented by appreciable oak flavour; the '78 had a little more acid and might last a little longer.

Rhine Riesling Spatlese 79: Lacks definition on bouquet — sweet, but that is all. The palate, too, lacks complexity but is very clean and the fruit flavour is attractive enough. May benefit from further bottle age.

Cabernet Sauvignon 1976: A gold medal winner. Has considerable varietal flavour and remarkable colour for a difficult wet vintage. Cabernet once again shows its ability to stand up to wet conditions.

Best buys
Hunter River Riesling 1979: $3.35
Chardonnay 1979: $3.65
Cabernet Sauvignon: $3.15

Cellaring potential: Chardonnay 2; Semillon 3–4 years; Rhine Riesling 1–2 years; Cabernet Sauvignon 5+ years.

Cellar door sales/facilities: Open Monday to Saturday 9 am to 5 pm; Sunday noon to 5 pm. Tasting facilities, BBQ and Rural Museum.

Retail distribution: Extensive New South Wales; limited elsewhere. Distributors are Walcie Pty Limited.

Summary: Hollydene became part of the Wyndham group in 1975 after a prolonged period of financial difficulty. The quality of the wines improved markedly after the acquisition, but Hollydene still has a fairly low marketing profile.

Horderns Wybong Estate

If I had a winery with one tenth of the charm and romance, or a vineyard situated in a valley half as beautiful, I don't think it would matter to me whether my wines were good, bad or indifferent. Now I am perfectly certain that co-owners Dr Bob Smith (normally a Sydney orthopaedic surgeon) and Denman grazier David Hordern do care a great deal about the quality of all the wines. It is pure coincidence that some are very good and others are not.

Happily, the dip in quality seems to have been halted. It was, I feel sure, due to some infected oak barrels which gave rise to a foxy/cheesy character in some of the intermediate year wines. The younger vintages show a return to the superb form of that magic '74 Semillon with 2 trophies and innumerable gold medals under its belt — the last as recently as the '79 Hunter Valley Show.

Established: 1965.

Address: Brogheda Station, Wybong via Muswellbrook, 2333. (065) 47 8127.

Winemakers: Dr Bob Smith, John Hordern.

Annual crush: 100 tonnes.

Horderns Wybong Estate

HUNTER VALLEY 1980
SEMILLON

Made from selected semillon grapes grown on the sandy loam slopes of Wybong Estate and wood aged to achieve the style of a French white burgundy, while retaining classic 'Hunter' characteristics.

Bottle No. 2001   of 6000

PRODUCT OF AUSTRALIA   750 ml

Horderns Wybong Estate

HUNTER VALLEY
BENGALA, Burgundy Style

Made from 100% Shiraz grapes, cold fermented like a premium white wine to produce a soft light bodied beaujolais type wine excellent for drinking either chilled or at room temperature.

Bottle No.

PRODUCT OF AUSTRALIA   750 ml

Principal wines/wine styles

Personal selection Semillon '79: Full, rich fruit character on both bouquet and palate with a hint of the banana yeast character found on many current Australian whites. Has considerable depth and will unquestionably age very well.

Semillon 1978: A wine with considerable overall flavour, yet somewhat austere. The fruit has an apple/malic tang and needs to fill out on the middle palate. The balance is good between oak, fruit and acid so that it should come together well with a little more time in bottle.

Semillon Vat 4, 1974: Lovely green/gold colour. Classic Hunter aroma of honeyed burnt toast. Superb palate: long flavoured, complex and yet with fresh acid to the finish. At its top; cannot be faulted.

Bengala Light Red: Named after the 140 year old stone prison removed from Bengala and re-erected as the winery in 1969. A light, easy drinking red with definite Hunter character but pleasant fruit flavour lingering on the finish.

A wide range of Rhine Riesling, Traminer and Traminer Riesling blends, together with mature reds, are also available.

Cellaring potential: The '74 Semillon establishes a minimum 6 year span for the best wines of this variety; aromatic varietals 1–2 years; reds of indeterminate span according to quality.

Cellar door sales/facilities: Open Monday to Saturday 10 am to 4 pm; Sunday noon to 4 pm. BBQ and camping facilities.

Retail distribution: Very limited. Camperdown Cellars, Sydney.

Summary: At the time of writing 11 wines were on offer ranging back to 1976 at a maximum price of $36 a dozen, with the majority at $30 per dozen. At these levels it is an open invitation to try the wines and see for yourself, for price is no barrier. The winery is a compulsory stop for anyone visiting the Upper Hunter.

3 Mt Dangar Vineyards

Yet another new name on the wine map of the Hunter, although the vineyard has been a major producer of grapes since 1969. Originally a joint venture, The Adelaide Steamship Company Limited (a company with a catholic taste in investments if there ever was one) became sole owner in 1975.

The vineyard has always had a high reputation for the quality of the grapes, due in part to the skill and dedication of its manager, Dick Hilder. As part of a major re-alignment of supply arrangements, Mt Dangar ceased selling grapes to Rosemount and took a joint share in the Denman Estate winery in 1979.

In that year, well over 1000 tonnes of grapes were crushed, and most of the wine was sold in bulk to old-established Hunter wineries. About eight per cent was held and bottled for release under the Mt Dangar label, offered principally to the shareholders in Adelaide Steamship. The success of that offering resulted in an even greater retention in 1980, although the total crush was only a third of that of the year before due to the drought.

Established: 1968.
Address: Highway 84 at Sandy Hollow, NSW, 2333.
(065) 47 4504.
Winemaker: Ian Scarborough (Scarmac Pty Limited).
Annual crush: 1000 tonnes.
Annual sales: 7000 cases (most wine sold in bulk).
Principal wines/wine styles

Chablis 1979: Pale colour, with some bottling SO_2 still evident. Crisp, clean and nice firm finish. In Chablis style.

Hunter River Riesling 1979: Pleasant medium-weight fruit. Faint trace of dirt both on bouquet and palate.

Hunter River White Burgundy 1979: Big, full, clean bouquet. Good full fruity palate with nice balance. Very much in style.

Traminer 1979: Very light on both nose and palate. Innocuous drinking.

Traminer Riesling 1979: Full, rich fruity aroma. Plenty of character and already showing optimum development. Above average commercial style.

Hermitage 1979: A wine which sold out literally overnight. Low alcohol and fresh when released but already seems a little tired.

Cabernet Sauvignon 1979: Intense, ripe-flavoured Cabernet, a trophy winner at 1979 Hunter Valley Show.

Best buys: White Burgundy '79: $2.10
Traminer Riesling: $2.40
Cabernet Sauvignon '79: $2.75 (released July 1980)

Cellaring potential: Drink-now styles.

Cellar door sales/facilities: Open 9–5 Monday to Saturday.

Retail distribution: Nil. The sale of bottled wine is intended to remain low key — second fiddle to the production and sale of bulk wine.

Summary: The shareholders of Adelaide Steamship received an unusual bonus in 1979 in receiving first offer of these extremely modestly priced wines. 1980 should see even better wines (for release September 1980).

CC Queldinburg

With Kevin Sobels' South Australian background (he grew up, and worked as winemaker for some years, in the Barossa–Watervale area) it is not surprising that he elected to build a winery which relies entirely on bought-in grapes. This pattern is as common in South Australia as it is rare in the Hunter Valley.

The first vintage was in 1974, and in the following years Sobels has established a reputation as a maker of distinctive varietal wines. The Traminers are probably the best, but some full-flavoured Semillons and flavoursome oak-matured Shiraz have also been released over the past 12 months and have been well received.

Established: 1974.

Address: New England Highway, 1.5 km south of Muswellbrook (PO Box 317, Muswellbrook). (065) 432 939.

Winemaker: Kevin Sobels.
Principal wines/wine styles
Rhine Riesling '79: Pleasant lemony Rhine Riesling aroma. Full, fresh fruity palate with some residual sugar. Attractive, easy-drinking style in highly commercial mould.
Traminer 1979: Fruity, aromatic wine of medium depth, not at all heavy. Elegant, light, refreshing wine, with trace of hardness on the finish — part of so many Australian Traminers, it seems — the only criticism.
Cabernet Sauvignon 1977: Colour suggesting some development; trace of browning. Very attractive sappy Cabernet bouquet; St. Emilion overtones. Elegant "cool" style; most appealing.

Shiraz 1976: Rich, soft bouquet with obvious but very well handled oak. As with the Cabernet, obvious signs of development, but nice touch of tannin on finish gives reassurance.
Best buys
Rhine Riesling 1979: $3.50
Traminer 1979: $3.90
Cabernet Sauvignon 1977: $3.50
(Prices retail May 1980)
Cellaring potential: White wines 1–3 years; reds 4–6 years.
Cellar door sales/facilities: Open Monday to Saturday 8.30 am to 5 pm; Sunday noon to 5 pm. Full tasting facilities.
Retail distribution: Distributed by The Stone Wine Company, 55 Albert Street, Leichhardt, Sydney. Reasonable coverage of New South Wales.
Summary: Kevin Sobels is a professional winemaker and seldom slips in the production of a range of red, white and semi-sweet white wines from Upper Hunter grapes.

A Richmond Grove

Richmond Grove has had a fairytale rise to success in a few short years and in a market which in most areas suffered from oversupply. The reasons for its success are the careful selection of grape varieties, some very good winemaking and astute marketing. Outstanding success in the show ring, while arousing a certain amount of controversy, has put the icing on the cake.

Only white varieties have been planted in this 100 hectare vineyard situated south of Sandy Hollow. These include Chardonnay, Traminer, Rhine Riesling, Sauvignon Blanc, and Semillon. The wines are released principally under varietal names but Chablis and White Burgundy generic styles are also made. A single label and a single recommended retail price have been adopted. The wines have had an enviable run of success in blind tastings organised by trade and wine magazine sources.

The grapes from the vineyard are processed at the Hollydene winery, but are kept totally separate from those of Hollydene, and are made in a somewhat different fashion. The differences stem from the views of Rhinecastle, who are sole distributors of the wines and who provide a wealth of marketplace experience.

Established: 1977.
Location: Due south of Sandy Hollow off Denman Road.
Winemaker: Barry Platt.
Annual sales: 40 000 cases.
Principal wines/wine styles
Chardonnay 1979: Clean, gentle fruit bouquet, with obvious varietal character but without intense ripe fig–peach character

sometimes encountered. Medium bodied palate, fresh and well balanced. Seemingly much less luscious than the show wines, although there is a hint of underlying sweetness.
Chablis 1979: In common with all the releases of this vintage, the major impression is of clean, fresh fruit. Quite soft on the middle palate but finishes firm and bone dry as befits the style.
White Burgundy 1979: A Semillon-Chardonnay blend, full and flavoursome which fits as perfectly into the requirements of the style as does the Chablis. Seems headed for rapid development and should be at its peak in the 2 years following vintage.
Gewurztraminer 1979: A blood brother to the Wyndham

Gewurtz, but with less sugar (although it still has appreciable sweetness). Very aromatic fruity bouquet, with varietal flavour absolutely unmistakable. Excellent acid to finish keeps a generous wine in balance. First class early drinking style.

Sauvignon Blanc (late picked) 1979: Interesting varietal bouquet — chalky herbaceous, a striking counterpoint to the luscious, sweet palate. A traditional, French treatment of a variety which, if made dry, often produces featureless wines in Australia.

Best buys: Any one of the above wines at the common recommended retail price of $3.40

Cellaring potential: With the (qualified) exception of the Chardonnay all should be close to their best within 1 to 3 years of vintage.

Cellar door sales: Nil.

Retail distribution: Extensive, particularly in New South Wales and Victoria. Distributed by Rhinecastle Wines.

Summary: After a troubled first vintage in 1977, Richmond Grove has gone from strength to strength and now offers the best white varietals from the Upper Hunter.

Rosemount Estates

When most other companies were struggling for survival, Rosemount was going from strength to strength. Its penetration of the market between '75 and '78 is a success story unlikely to be repeated, and the company has a seemingly secure base underpinned by consistently imaginative and effective advertising campaigns.

It began as a sideline in a mixed stud-farming operation of New Guinea plantation-owner Bob Oatley (a companion in that respect of Bob Roberts of Huntington Estate). The early wines (its first vintage was in 1975) were of remarkable quality and caused havoc in wine shows.

In more recent years, Rosemount has struggled to retain that quality while meeting the seemingly insatiable demands of the market place. In a remarkable David and Goliath encounter, it acquired Wybong from Penfolds at the end of 1977 and has since purchased the Roxburgh Vineyard from Denman Estate, as well as establishing a number of new vineyards of its own.

The current whites (from 1979, a marvellous vintage in both Lower and Upper Hunter) are generally pleasant wines if not subjected to close scrutiny. At the time of writing, a good 1975 Cabernet Sauvignon was still available at a modest price, stressing the difficulty which most of the Upper Hunter makers have in selling their reds. This is a wine which unfairly suffers from the reputation of many of its brothers from the area.

Established: 1969.
Address: Rosemount Road, Denman, 2328, 8 km west of township. (065) 47 2467.
Winemaker: Mark Turnbull.
Annual crush: 2500 tonnes (group crush).
Principal wines/wine styles:
Rhine Riesling: Light and delicate style with good balance, seldom reaching great heights but always pleasant. Intermittent releases of special show reserve stock of wines of much more character and body are worth watching for.
Traminer: Gently spicy wines, usually pale in colour (particularly

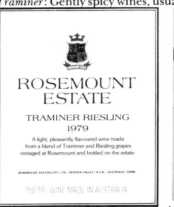
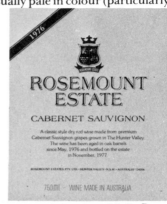

when young). Soft in flavour and relatively low in acid. Reflects very high yields in the vineyard. The 1979 showed better flavour with pleasant lemony acid on the finish.
Traminer Riesling: Rosemount was one of the early birds with this very successful blend. There is no question the flavours of the two grapes do complement each other well. In recent years Rosemount seems to have used particularly light base-material and relied on a trace of residual sugar to help. In fact a commercially successful formula and at a bland level, pleasant enough.
Semillon: Clean, light wines of good balance but minimal varietal flavour when young. Do benefit from a few years bottle age.
Semillon Chardonnay: Some very disappointing wines for a potentially good blend, although others have liked the '79 more than I did.
Chardonnay: Extremely disappointing in 1979.
Hermitage: As so often happens, the reds are entirely ignored, but are inherently as good if not better than the whites. The Hermitages are usually soft, round wines in the light style certainly, but with a nice touch of new oak and ready to drink when released with 3 to 4 years bottle age.
Cabernet Sauvignon: Similar to the Hermitage but rather better.

Undoubtedly on the soft side and with camphor-oak flavour a little dominant, but very pleasant mature red wine at 4 years of age.

Best buys: Traminer 1979: $3.57

Rhine Riesling 1979: $3.57

Cabernet Sauvignon 1976: $3.95

Cellaring potential: Very little: all wines released ready for drinking.

Cellar door sales/facilities: Open 10 am to 4 pm Monday to Friday; noon to 4 pm Saturday. Full tasting facilities.

Retail distribution: National.

Summary: Rosemount produces a range of white varietals which provide uncomplicated and pleasant drinking. It will have to think again if it wishes to get back into the top quality end of the market, but there is evidence to suggest it is doing just that.

Segenhoe

One of a number of Hunter vineyards to have suffered near mortal wounds in the collapse of the red-wine market in the 1970s. Poor winemaking did not help a cumbersome, syndicated, joint ownership of 230 individuals, and the operation never looked like being a success.

Salvation came late in 1978 when Tyrrells entered into a long-term lease of the winery and contracted to purchase the output of the vineyard. With Tyrrells' expertise, the quality of the Segenhoe wines was lifted immediately and some very good '79 whites were released.

I would expect that, in common with most Upper Hunter vineyards, the emphasis will remain heavily in favour of the aromatic white styles. It is also a fair assumption that most of the production will find its way through to Tyrrell and possibly other labels.

Established: 1970.

Address: Near Glenbawn Dam, Aberdeen, 2336 (PO Box 1077, GPO Sydney). (065) 43 7274.

Winemaker: Allan Knapp.

Annual crush: 1100 tonnes.

Principal wines/wine styles

Rhine Riesling '79: Big, full-flavoured wine with hint of H_2S on bouquet. Stacks of flavour on palate; rich, full style supported by a degree of residual sugar.

Traminer '79: Archetypal, full, rich, spicy Traminer. Made quite dry; has a touch of the hardness endemic to the variety, but very good wine of its type.

Chardonnay '79: Rich bouquet verging on fatness. Excellent fruit flavour with good varietal definition on palate. Medium depth; only needs a touch of good oak to lift it even further.

White Burgundy '79: Semillon-based wine. Bouquet rather dumb. Palate very much better; fruity, smooth and round. An easy-drinking wine of good white Burgundy style.

Best buys: Rhine Riesling: $2.50
Traminer: $3.25
White Burgundy: $2.25
Chardonnay: $3.75

Cellaring potential: All basically drink-now styles; Chardonnay could benefit from further 12 months in bottle.

Cellar door sales/tasting facilities: Open Monday to Saturday 9 am to 4 pm. Tasting facilities.

Retail Distribution: Wines marketed primarily to the several hundred shareholders in Chateau Douglas. Retail outlets few, but include Sunnybrook Cellars, 4 Bridge Street, Sydney.

Summary: Limited quantities of vastly improved Segenhoe white varietal wines are available, but the main output will be marketed by Tyrrells and an associated vineyard. Previously known as Chateau Douglas.

BC Verona

Verona started life as a sideline to the irrigation-equipment business of owner Keith Yore, but as so often happens, it tended to take over. The familiar pattern of Upper Hunter vineyards repeats: the reds are light-bodied and inconsequential; the whites — particularly the aromatic varietals Rhine Riesling and Traminer — are much better. Verona adds Chardonnay and smaller quantities of Semillon.

Established: 1971.
Address: New England Highway, Muswellbrook, on northern outskirts of township (PO Box 217, Muswellbrook, 2333) (065) 431 055.
Winemaker: Rod Upton.
Principal wines/wine styles
Gewurtztraminer: Is noteworthy for the amount of flavour, particularly for the Upper Hunter. The wines come on fairly quickly in bottle and are at their best about 2 years from vintage.
Rhine Riesling: Also fairly full-flavoured, but with good balance.
Chardonnay: Still made in very restricted quantities as plantings come into bearing. The 1979 vintage was one of the best from the Upper Hunter. Has abundant flavour on middle palate and good acid on finish. Trace of H_2S on bouquet only possible criticism.
Valdepenas: A Spanish variety and the only table wine (to my knowledge) made in Australia from this variety.
Best buys
1979 (or 1980) Chardonnay: $3.00
1979 (or 1980) Gewurtztraminer: $3.00

(prices current April 1980 for 1979 vintage).
Cellaring potential: With exception of Chardonnay (2–3 years) essentially drink-now styles; reds also on release which have 3–5 years bottle age and are therefore mature.
Cellar door sales/facilities: Open Monday to Saturday 10 am to 6 pm; noon to 6 pm Sunday. Tasting and BBQ facilities.
Retail distribution: Through eastern States by AML and F.
Summary: A fairly small-scale operation by Upper Hunter standards, providing white varietals with greater-than usual flavour. Chardonnay very good, and Traminer above average.

Mudgee

Of all the "new" areas of New South Wales, Mudgee has to be the most exciting. I say "new" because grapes were first planted in the district in 1858, and there has been at least one winery in operation at all times since. However, the real growth has come over the past ten years, as old vineyards have been resuscitated and new ones established.

In this, Mudgee has been lucky, it seems. Broad-acre plantings by large wine companies did not occur; rather, the accent was on small acreages of premium varieties, with careful matching of soil and aspect with variety. Most of the vineyards are at high altitudes, varying between 500 and 600 metres above sea level. Thus, although the district is as far north as the Hunter Valley, its harvest is some six to seven weeks later.

Spring frost is sometimes a problem, and caused substantial crop losses in the '80 vintage. Rain, however, is seldom the scourge that it is in the Hunter Valley at vintage time, because Mudgee is on the inland side of the Great Dividing Range. The disturbances which bedevil the Hunter are usually coastal, and reasonably dry vintages are the order of the day.

The vines grow with considerable vigour and produce ample yields (one to two or more tonnes per hectare) without irrigation. The soils are basically red loam interspersed with limestone and ironstone, an ideal growing medium. The heavy clay subsoils retain moisture, a distinct help, given the fairly low 600 mm rainfall.

Mudgee whites and reds are notable for their varietal fruit flavour. There is a considerable range of white wine styles made, although overall plantings are heavily weighted towards red wines. Virtually all vineyards have some Chardonnay, and most are in the course of increasing their plantings. Craigmoor has the oldest and largest area of Chardonnay (among a considerable number of other varieties). It is significant that when Craigmoor's long-serving winemaker, Pieter van Gent left to establish his own vineyard, he was to specialize in Chardonnay.

Craigmoor, Huntington and Montrose have all produced Chardonnays of special distinction. There is no question about the class of this grape, and although it is neither immune to district influences nor to indifferent winemaking, its peach–

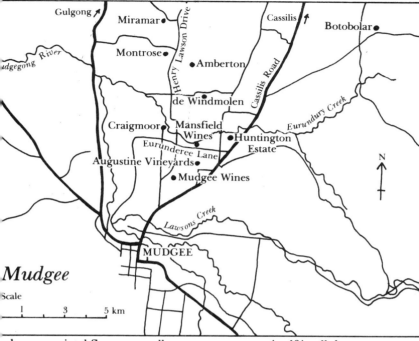

Mudgee

Scale

1   3   5 km

honey varietal flavour usually manages to assert itself in all the Mudgee wines.

Semillon has nowhere near the dominant position it assumes in the Hunter Valley. Some interesting wines have been made with varying degrees of residual sugar, from the high-quality, full-blown, Sauterne-style Bemosa sweet white of Montrose, through to the faintly sweet Semillon of Huntington. This reflects the cooler ripening conditions which make for this kind of treatment.

The full gamut of aromatic varietals are represented. Traminers of particular class come from Amberton, Botobolar and Craigmoor; Botolobar offers Marsanne and Amberton has released a Sauvignon Blanc. The high-point of these styles, however, is in my view the Rhine Rieslings of Botobolar and Miramar. The former is an extremely good wine; the latter another thing again, with the greatest degree of intense Germanic-lime flavour I have seen from a wine outside the Rhine for many years.

Shiraz is a total enigma. In a number of the vineyards (notably Huntington and Botobolar) it seems as if it is determined to out-Hunter the Hunter, with a heavy, cowshed, sweaty-saddle character. Suggestions of H_2S are strenuously denied by winemakers Roberts and Wahlquist, who point to their absolutely clean Cabernets and assure me they treat both wines the same way and they regularly use the copper test treatment.

Yet other Shiraz — notably that of Montrose and Burnbrae — is soft, spicy and above all, clean. The only logical explanation is that soil and microclimate must play a particular role in some of the vineyards.

The noble red is undoubtedly Cabernet, which in the hands of virtually all makers produces a deeply coloured, rich and well-balanced wine. The style seems rounder and sweeter — without the intense herbaceous–leaf character of some districts — which would no doubt suit most palates, anyway. (Those light, green Cabernets are something of an acquired taste.)

Mudgee is the first Australian wine district to introduce a full-scale appellation system covering all the commercial wineries — if one accepts that the scheme is a voluntary one. (The Mt Barker–Margaret River areas of Western Australia were first to try such a scheme, but it has remained on an experimental basis.)

The Mudgee scheme provides not only an absolute guarantee that the fruit and wine is of Mudgee origin, but also a significant amount of reassurance on the quality of the wine. All wines are tasted and assessed by a panel of winemakers under show conditions. If the wines show clear winemaking faults or are obviously out of style, appellation will be denied.

I have yet to see a poor wine with the appellation sticker; I have seen a number of poor wines without it. Its absence (or for that matter its presence) is, however, not conclusive, for participation is purely voluntary.

The Society for the APPELLATION of the Wines of MUDGEE Certificate № 1 8 4 Bottle № 0 0 1 8 2 4

3 Amberton Wines

Amberton Wines is one of the newest arrivals on the Mudgee scene, with 1979 marking the first vintage of commercial consequence.

Amberton is the brainchild — lovechild might be a better term — of Manuel Damien (a well known Sydney restaurateur) and a group of wine and food-loving doctors who frequent Damien's restaurant, The Little Snail.

The first plantings were made in 1975, and the vineyard has expanded progressively since. 21 hectares are presently under vine and it is planned to plant a further 4 hectares of Chardonnay in 1981. At that stage the principal varieties will be Chardonnay, Semillon, Shiraz and Cabernet, with lesser areas of Rhine Riesling, Sauvignon Blanc and Traminer. 100 hectares of land suitable for planting are available, with an expected yield of 6 to 7 tonnes per hectare at vine maturity.

The '79 vintage was made for Amberton by Pieter Van Gent and is a credit to both vineyard and winemaker. An entirely new winery with a 300 tonne capacity was constructed for the '80 vintage and is replete with all the now essential gadgetry for high quality white and red wine making. The owners are extremely proud of their 1980 vintage wines; and if they are better than the '79s, they will be well worth seeking out.

Established: 1975.

Address: Henry Lawson Drive, Mudgee 2850, north of town and 2 km past Lawson Memorial.

Winemaker: John Rozentals.

Annual crush: 82 tonnes 1980 (estate grown) ultimately increasing to 200+ tonnes.

Principal wines/wine styles

Rhine Riesling Traminer 1979: Full, heavy almost Alsatian style with some SO_2 showing. Flavoursome palate with Traminer dominant and firm finish.

Traminer 1979: Clear, spicy Traminer with 'oily' overtones. Made totally dry and all the more interesting for that. A well above average, full flavoured wine.

Semillon Chardonnay Sauvignon Blanc 1979: A total fruit salad style no doubt due to very limited quantities of fruit. Semillon and Sauvignon Blanc dominant. Quite heavy style.

Chardonnay 1979: Strong oak overlay but varietal character discernable. Oak also dominates palate, but should come at least partially into balance with bottle age.

Shiraz Cabernet 1978: Touch of H_2S, or is this simply a Shiraz district character? Medium bodied with some astringency on finish. Needs time.

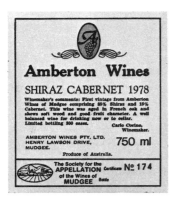

Cellaring potential: Aromatic varietal whites 1-2 years; Chardonnay 3+ years. Red wine styles not yet known.

Best buys

1979 vintage will undoubtedly be sold out by now. 1980 vintage wines will be:

1979 Cabernet Shiraz (350 cases)

1980 Semillon 45% (1000 cases)

1980 Semillon (450 cases)

1980 Traminer (250 cases)

1980 Rhine Riesling, Semillon and Sauvignon Blance (late picked) (450 cases)

Prices not fixed at time of writing; those for '79 vintage ranged between $3.00 and $3.50 a bottle.

Cellar door sales/facilities: Open 9.30 am to 5.30 pm Monday to Saturday. Noon to 5.30 pm Sunday. Tasting facilities.

Retail distribution: New South Wales and ACT: I H Baker & Co.

Victoria: Duke and Moorfield.

Mail orders welcome to Box 21, Randwick 2031.

Summary: Wines of impressive quality from a new vineyard. The future direction will be watched with considerable interest.

DD Augustine Vineyards

Augustine is the re-incarnation of a vineyard established by Dr Fiaschi around the turn of the century, and which had been abandoned in the 1940s. It shares the high altitude of virtually all Mudgee vineyards and the relatively late ripening patterns. The emphasis is on production of straight varietal wines, with a Traminer–Riesling blend the only exception to this pattern.

Quality is variable: I have seen one or two very poor wines, and I suspect problems exist with the handling of some of the small oak casks in use. Other wines are much better, with the range extending from positively flavoured Traminers through to rich, dark and tannic Cabernets.

Established: 1918

Address: Airport Road, Mudgee, 2850, 7 km north-east of township. (063) 72 1536.

Winemakers: Peter & Ken Spencer.

Annual crush: 200 tonnes.

Annual sales: 15,000 cases.

Principal wines/wine styles

A number of straight varietal wines are usually available: Chardonnay, Traminer, Cabernet Sauvignon, Pinot Noir and Shiraz. The range also extends to several varietal blends (Traminer Riesling and Pinot Riesling) and to generic styles such as White Burgundy and Moselle Superior.

Chardonnay '79 was a very disappointing wine, flat hard and lacking in fruit flavour.

Cabernet Sauvignon: Very much better, both the '76 & '77 showing good flavour

Best buys

Cabernet Sauvignon 1977: $2.95

Cellaring potential: Traminer and Traminer Riesling, 1–2 years; Chardonnay, 2–4 years; Cabernet Sauvignon, 3–6 years.

Retail distribution: Limited retail distribution Sydney (Great Australian Wine Company, 35a Willoughby Road, Crows Nest) and Brisbane. Mail orders readily accepted.

Summary: A relatively small vineyard producing wines of variable quality but always with pronounced flavour.

B Botobolar

Flaxed-haired, blue-eyed and broad-shouldered – Gil Wahlquist is everyone's idea of what a viking chief should look like; his approach to winemaking and the Mudgee area in general seem to fit neatly into the same mould.

He has long ago banned the use of all pesticides and weedicides in his vineyard; only mild fungicides are permitted. Insects, birds, animals and other plants (including weeds bearing exotic names such as 'hyssop' and 'penny royal') are all encouraged in a symbiotic relationship with the vines, each balancing and at times supporting the others.

An ex-journalist, Wahlquist is a tireless ambassador for the Mudgee area, a driving force behind the Mudgee Appellation Scheme and publisher of a periodical, *Botobolar Bugle,* (which does not hesitate to mention other growers and their wines).

It comes almost as an afterthought to say that he makes a range of very good — and at times unusual and very appealing — wines. They need no support from conservationists or ecologists and stand easily on their own merits.

Established: 1970.

Address: Botobolar Lane, Mudgee, 18 km north-east of town (PO Box 212, Mudgee, 2850). (063) 73 3840.

Winemaker: Gil Wahlquist.

Annual crush: 150 tonnes estate grown; 5 tonnes bought in.

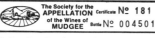

Principal wine/wine styles

Marsanne: The only grower of this variety in the district. Positive fruity flavour with good varietal definition — unusual though the variety is.

Rhine Riesling: Usually one of Botobolar's top wines. The 1979 had a dazzling green-gold colour, quite superb, with stacks of flavour on the middle palate balanced by excellent acid on the finish.

Chardonnay: Made in small quantities and quickly sells out. Tropical fruit flavours are attractive, although there have been one or two oak handling problems.

Budgee Budgee: A wine as unusual as its name suggests. A sweet white made from Shiraz, White Muscat and Black Muscat it has a unique and by no means unpleasant fruit-pastille aroma and taste.

Crouchen: Another unusual grape for the district, and produces a very popular, spicy white.

Shiraz/Hermitage: Variously labelled in an effort to lure customers to the wine, but often very good. Clear, fresh and fruity, these are very well made and usually have the benefit of three or four years bottle age when released.

Cabernet Sauvignon: A ready seller. Excellent purple colour, and, like the Shiraz, made to preserve fruit freshness and varietal flavour. The 1978 has very good balance between fruit, tannin and acid and should develop very well in bottle.

Best buys
1979 Rhine Riesling: $3.00
1978 Cabernet Sauvignon: $3.95
1977 Hermitage: $2.40

Cellaring potential: Aromatic whites (Rhine Riesling, Marsanne, Traminer, Crouchen) for early consumption. Hermitage/Shiraz, 3–5 years; Cabernet Sauvignon 4–6+ years.

Cellar door sales/facilities: Open 9 am to 5 pm Monday to Saturday; noon to 5 pm Sunday. Tasting Facilities. Bulk sales (25 litre containers) as well as bottles. BBQ's by arrangement. Vineyard tour by appointment.

Retail distribution: Principally cellar door and mail order (inquiries and orders welcome) but also stocked by the Oak Barrell, 154 Elizabeth Street, Sydney.

Summary: In Gil Wahlquist's words, "The philosophy of the winery is to produce wines which reflect the character of the soil and the countryside. The wines are not made to suit a preconceived idea of what a wine should taste like".

Burnbrae

One of the newer and smaller Mudgee vineyards, the wines of which are not well known but which certainly do nothing to impair the reputation of Mudgee. Part owner and winemaker Paul Tumminello is a Bachelor of Agricultural Science from Sydney University and spent the '75 vintage working with Gil Wahlquist. He is also a dedicated, if not fanatical, wine student who regularly attends comparative tastings of Australian and European wines. I have no doubt that this open minded approach can only benefit a winemaker and that it shows in the major release so far made by Burnbrae — a '77 Cabernet Shiraz Malbec, which has a gold medal to its credit.

The scale of operations is still tiny: the Malbec component of that wine came from 130 vines. Eight hectares of Shiraz, Cabernet, Rhine Riesling, Semillon, Trebbiano and Chardonnay are in bearing, with a further three hectares coming into bearing. Four hectares of black muscat planted many years ago remain.

Established: 1971. (Winery 1976).

Address: The Hargraves Road, Eurunderee via Mudgee. (02) 86 3704.

Winemaker: Paul Tumminello.

Annual crush: 18 tonnes (1980) (increasing to 90 tonnes).

Annual sales: 700 cases.

Principal wines/wine styles

Cabernet Shiraz Malbec 1977: Very clean wine with lots of fruit but yet to fully open up on bouquet. A very smooth and long flavoured wine with fruit dominant rather than oak. Good finish to a good wine.

Dry White 1979: 40% Chardonnay (Bronze Medal winner).

Due for release July 1980: *Cabernet Shiraz* 1978, *Muscat Liqueur* 1979 and *Vintage Port* 1979.

Cellaring potential: Red wines 4 to 8 years. Fortifieds longer.

Best buys: Cabernet Shiraz Malbec 1977 $3.20

Cabernet Shiraz 1978 $3.20

Cellar door sales/facilities: Open Monday to Saturday 8 am to 5 pm; Sunday noon to 6 pm.

Retail distribution: Camperdown Cellars Sydney sole stockists plus various restaurants. Mail orders welcome to P Tumminello, 15 High Street, Epping.

Summary: A vineyard still on the way up; clearly capable of making some very good wines.

BB Craigmoor

Craigmoor is by far the oldest vineyard in Mudgee, and is also the best known. Its products are distributed extensively throughout New South Wales, although they are less well known in other States.

Over recent years, increasing emphasis has been placed on the production and marketing of a wide range of varietal wines. More recently still, under the direction of winemaker Ian Lindeman, Craigmoor has undertaken a number of interesting experiments with the use of new small oak. As well as a wood-matured Semillon of very considerable flavour and style from the '79 vintage, three Chardonnays matured respectively in French, German and American oak were released.

Craigmoor has retained significant quantities of some of its older whites and reds, and progressively releases small parcels of these. They add interest to a range of very good wines, and also give an insight into cellaring potential of the usually young wines coming from this district.

Established: 1858.

Address: Eurunderee Lane, Mudgee, 5 km north of town (PO Box 67, Mudgee, 2850).

Winemaker: Ian Lindeman.

Principal wines/wine styles:

Semillon: Craigmoor has also been experimenting, with considerable success, in wood-matured Semillons. Rich and complex.

Traminer: The positive flavour of the variety is given free rein, but, despite the very considerable volume of spicy flavour, the wines avoid oiliness when young. Drink-now style.

Sauvignon Blanc: Not surprisingly, a lighter and firmer style from a variety which seems to adapt uncomfortably to Australian conditions.

Semillon Chardonnay: Some re-releases of older vintages prove the worth of this blend (although the Semillon dominates) and also of the area generally as a cellaring proposition.

Chardonnay: One of the most consistently good Chardonnays from the district, released since 1971. After a hiatus, all the wine is now oak-matured with a variety of oaks employed. Very full-flavoured and generous wines leaving no doubt at all about their parentage.

Shiraz: The marketplace turns its back on the variety and some lovely mature wines at ludicrously low prices result. Soft, yet rich fruit is a hallmark of the Craigmoor style.

Cabernet Sauvignon: A model of consistency. Craigmoor Cabernet is unquestionably of the richer, mouthfilling style, fleshed out even further by clever oak handling. No austerity here, and the wines develop a great depth of flavour over a 4–5 year span.

Best buys: Craigmoor Chardonnay 1979: $4.50
Craigmoor Semillon 1979: $4.50
Craigmoor Cabernet Sauvignon 1976: $4.00
Craigmoor Eurunderee Shiraz 1975: $3.75

Cellaring potential: Aromatic white varietals for immediate drinking; Semillon and Semillon Chardonnay blends, 2–5 years; Chardonnay, 3–8+ years; Cabernet and Shiraz, 3–6 years.

Cellar door sales/facilities: Open 8 am to 5 pm Monday to Saturday. Winetasting and winery tours. Extensive BBQ/picnic facilities.

Retail distribution: Reasonably extensive NSW. Cellar door/ mail order sales most important. Inquiries and orders welcome.

Summary: The senior citizen of Mudgee, as well as producing traditional reds and whites, is showing a willingness to innovate, and as a result has the widest range of wines of varying ages to be found in Mudgee.

XD de Windmolen

De Windmolen is one of the newest wineries in the Mudgee district, but its winemaker, Pieter van Gent, is one of the old hands. Before starting de Windmolen with the '79 vintage, van Gent had been chief winemaker at Craigmoor for many years after a ten-year stint at Penfolds.

Van Gent is a professional winemaker (in the minority at Mudgee) and will undoubtedly make use of the unlimited potential of the district's grapes. The initial offerings from the vineyard are a pot-pourri, but the range will always be limited, with emphasis on the production of wood-matured Chardonnay. Other Chardonnays from the district leave little doubt about the potential quality of this wine.

Established: 1979.
Address: Black Springs Road, Mudgee, 2850. 8 km north-east

of township. (063) 733 807.

Winemaker: Pieter van Gent.

Annual crush: 100–200 tonnes.

Principal wines/wine styles

Chardonnay: Style and quality yet to assert itself, but undoubtedly will. Poor wood contributed to a very mediocre '79 vintage, flat and oxidized.

Mudgee Shiraz 1979.

Angelic White: Sweet table wine.

Pipeclay port.

Pipeclay Vermouth: Italian style.

Cellar door sales/facilities: Open 9 am to 5 pm Monday to Saturday. Tasting room seats 28 people in choir stalls.

Retail distribution: Great Australian Wine Company, Crows Nest, Sydney; Bondi Junction Liquor Store, Sydney; Templestowe Cellars, Melbourne; Chesser Cellars, Adelaide; selected stores, Perth; Cellar door/mailing list sales welcome.

Summary: Newly established. No track record. Initial releases do not do the winemaker justice.

Huntington Estate

Bob and Wendy Roberts run one of the most impressive family winery operations in Australia. Their first plantings were in 1969; their first vintage in 1973, and Bob Roberts is an entirely self-taught winemaker without formal qualifications (other than immense energy and enthusiasm), so Huntington Estate has come an extraordinary distance in a very short time.

Until recently, the emphasis was on red wines; these will continue to provide the bulk of production, but several interesting Semillons and Chardonnays have been released and are strongly recommended. It is with the Cabernet, Merlot and Pinot Noir reds that Huntington really comes into its own. Significant amounts of Shiraz are made, with a vineyard or district flavour which I do not like. (Others have no such reservations, and the wine sells well.)

The Cabernet and Cabernet Merlot wines are intensely flavoured and complex wines of exceptional colour and cellaring potential. Roberts handles his oak very well — all the wines receive extended, small-wood maturation — and this adds a further dimension to naturally rich flavours. The Pinot Noir is not infrequently blended with Cabernet — until recently this practice was regarded as a market eccentricity on the winemaker's part, but is now endorsed by no less a company than Seppelts.

Established: 1969.
Address: Cassilis Road, Mudgee, 10 km north-north-east of township (063) 733 825.
Winemaker: Bob Roberts.
Annual crush: 300 tonnes.
Annual sales: 15,000 cases plus bulk wine for home bottling.

Principal wines/wine styles

Chardonnay: 1979 was the first full-scale release, and Roberts was so impressed with the quality and structure of the fruit he decided not to give it oak maturation. Without debating this somewhat curious logic, the wine was extremely good and augers very well for future releases.

Semillon: A star-bright wine with excellent yellow-green colour and a great deal of smooth-structured flavour. Gains even further flavour complexity when made medium dry; a very interesting style.

Rose: Made medium-dry and labelled with an unexpected flight of fancy, the wine demonstrates Roberts' all-round winemaking skills and also the virtues of Mudgee fruit — very fresh, very clean and very good.

Shiraz: Made in both medium-bodied and full-bodied styles, usually exhibiting flavour characteristics far closer to Hunter Valley Hermitage than other Mudgee makers.

Cabernet Sauvignon: Consistently good-to-great wines of lovely colour, complex oak but, above all, rich Cabernet flavour. More refined and elegant than those of Craigmoor, but the fruit style is not dissimilar. Strongly recommended.

Cabernet Merlot: A classic Bordeaux blend made in very small quantities, but of extremely high quality. The '77 was the first release and sold out overnight.

Best buys
The 1980 releases should be available at the time of publication.
Semillon: $3.00
Cabernet Merlot 1978: $4.00
Cabernet MB 16: $3.50

Cellaring potential: Chardonnay 2–4 years; Semillon 1–2 years; Shiraz 3–5 years; Cabernet 5–7 years.

Cellar door sales/facilities: Open Monday to Friday 9 am to 5 pm; Saturdays 10 am to 1 pm, 2 pm to 5 pm; Sundays noon to 4 pm. Airconditioned tasting room.

Retail distribution: Very limited; virtually all sales cellar door and mail order. Inquiries/orders welcome.

Summary: Exceptionally well-made and very reasonably priced wines from one of Australia's most talented, self-made winemakers. Also specialises in high-quality home bottling wine.

Mansfield Wines

When Peter Mansfield established his vineyard in 1975, his great-great-grandfather would have undoubtedly approved. He was Andreas Kurtz, who commenced growing grapes in Mudgee in the 1860s after he arrived from Wurttemberg. Along with the Roth family, the Kurtz name is foremost in the viticultural history of Mudgee.

Peter Mansfield spent five years with his uncle, Alf Kurtz, at Mudgee Wines before purchasing land at Eurunderee and establishing 55 acres of vineyard planted to both table and dessert wine grapes. Mansfield Wines was off the ground with its initial '78 vintage, but then fire struck in October 1979 and destroyed all the maturing wine. Mansfield is now offering only fortified wines plus a Moselle and Shiraz, all bought in. He hopes to have his own wines on offer again in 1982.

Established: 1975.
Address: Eurunderee Lane, Mudgee, 7 km north of township. (063) 733 871.

Winemaker: Peter Mansfield.

Principal wines/wine styles

At present time a comprehensive range of fortified wines are offered in flagon ($3.80) and by the bottle ($1.70). These are normally supplemented by: Trebbiano, Dry White Bin1, Dry White Bin 2, Cabernet Sauvignon, Cabernet Shiraz and Dry Red.

Summary: One suspects that Mansfield Wines will always represent the old-school approach to winemaking and marketing and for that reason may add variety to the Mudgee scene.

AA Miramar

Miramar has swept all before it since its first vintage in 1977 and confirms the enormous potential of the Mudgee district. A joint venture between Ken Digby (a Sydney architect) and winemaker Ian McRae (Roseworthy trained), it aims to remain limited in production to ensure absolute quality control.

McRae clearly knows the secret of producing first-class Rose, a far more difficult task than most people realize. The 1978 Eurunderee Rose won a gold medal in Adelaide in Class 5 (dry) and a bronze medal in Class 6 (semi-sweet) at the same show, a noteworthy effort. This pales into insignificance, however, against the record of the 1979 which won five gold medals at national wine shows and the championship trophy for Roses at the 1979 Perth Show.

The 1979 Chardonnay Semillon was only a whisker behind, winning three gold medals in national shows, and just losing to Tyrrells' Chardonnay for the Perth Championship.

Wines on release include Chardonnay Semillon, Rhine Riesling, Moselle, Rose, Shiraz Cabernet and a Shiraz Port (another trophy winner — best fortified wine at 1979 Hunter Valley

Wine Show). In the January 1980 edition of *Winestate,* the 1979 Rhine Riesling, Chardonnay Semillon, and Rose were all named as wines of the year, a notable achievement.

Established: 1977.

Address: Henry Lawson Drive, Mudgee, 2850, north of town. (063) 733 874.

Winemaker: Ian McRae.

Annual crush: 30 tonnes estate grown; 75 tonnes bought in.

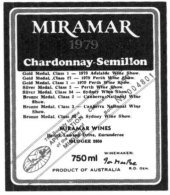

Principal wines/wine styles

Eurunderee Rose: The 1978 was a good wine, but the 1979 was clearly the best Rose made in Australia that year. Brilliant rose-pink colour, clear fresh fruit and cleansing acid on the finish are hallmarks of these superb drinking wines.

Rhine Riesling: Long, cool fermentation coupled with top class fruit result in very full-flavoured wines of intense germanic style with a spicy tang to the fruit flavour. Rather surprisingly, not many Rhine Rieslings are produced in Mudgee. The Miramar Rhine (1979 vintage) had astonishing total flavour.

Chardonnay Semillon: Very well-balanced, full flowery style with the peach-like flavour of the Chardonnay dominant, an unusual characteristic for such blends. The 1979 vintage was an exceptionally good wine.

Miramar Shiraz: A big, tannic style containing pressings material and given both old and new wood treatment. Deliberately made to be long-lived style.

Fortified wines: Several fortified wines are made.

Best buys

Eurunderee Rose: $2.75

Rhine Riesling: $4.15

Chardonnay Semillon: $3.50

(Prices current retail for 1979 vintage; '80 vintage will be higher.)

Cellaring potential: Rose, drink now; Rhine Riesling, 1–3 years; Chardonnay Semillon, 2–4 years; Shiraz 4–6+ years.
Cellar door sales/facilities: Open 9 am to 5 pm Monday to Saturday; noon to 5 pm Sunday.
Retail distribution: Very little. Great Australian Wine Company, Sydney. Cellar door sales/mail orders welcome.
Summary: An exciting new winery which has set a formidable standard with its early vintages and which will get better as the vines gain maturity. Very highly recommended.

BB | Montrose

Montrose is the largest winery in the Mudgee district, although it is a relative newcomer. Its modern building is very well equipped and under the direction of Italian-trained and qualified winemaker Carlo Corino, some extremely good and often quite different wines are made.

Corino has taken to Australia and Australians like a duck to water, but he brings an Italian touch to the vineyard's wines. This is particularly evident in the reds: Italian winemakers have a positive dislike of new oak flavour, prizing instead very old and large casks. The benefit is clearer and lighter fruit flavour, virtues apparent in the excellent 1977 Shiraz which was a Trophy winner at the Hunter Valley Wine Show in 1978.

Corino has also produced reds using the carbonic maceration fermentation technique; Chardonnay, both steel and oak matured (permissible for the variety, says Carlo); and an intensely flavoured Sauterne which received much favourable comment.
Established: 1974.
Address: Henry Lawson Drive, Mudgee, 8 km north of town (063) 73 3853.

Winemaker: Carlo Corino.

Annual crush: 300 tonnes.

Principal wines/wine styles

Chardonnay: Both stainless steel and oak matured styles made. The steel matured wine has intense varietal 'fig' flavour with appreciable fruit sweetness apparent on the palate, rather than the finish. Should have wide market appeal although judges who dislike sweetness in Chardonnay would not approve.

Semillon: Clean, full-flavoured wines with natural fruit flavour not obscured by oak.

Shiraz 1977: A first class wine of medium body highlighted by Rhone-like pepper/spice tang. Smooth and well balanced, it offers ideal drinking over the next one or two years.

Cabernet Sauvignon: Both conventionally made and carbonic maceration wines available. The latter has intense purple-blue colour, pronounced fruity flavour but is low in tannin and is quite light bodied. Designed for reasonably early drinking.

Bemosa Sauterne 1978: A luscious and complex sweet white wine which relied far more on genuinely late picked material and less on the addition of mistelle than most Australian Sauterne-style wines. It benefited accordingly.

Cellaring potential: All wines are made to be drunk young and fresh. 1–2 years for aromatic whites and 3–5 years for reds should represent maximum desirable cellaring range.

Best buys

Chardonnay 1979: $3.60

Chardonnay 1979 (wood matured): $3.90

Shiraz 1977: $2.90

All prices recommended retail as at May 1980.

Cellar door sales/facilities: Open Monday to Friday 8 am to 4.30 pm; Saturdays 11 am to 4 pm; Sundays noon to 4 pm. Cellar door sales and full fasting facilities.

Retail distribution: Distributed in New South Wales and Queensland by Montrose Wines; Victoria by Agostino & Co, The Cellar, Crittenden, Ritchies & Templestowe; Western Australia by Regional Vineyard Distributors, Fremantle.

Summary: Montrose wines deserve to be far better known. Their quality is extremely reliable and their style very much in keeping with the demands of the market place.

Mudgee Wines

Mudgee Wines was established by Alf Kurtz in the mid-60s, reviving a century old family tradition. Kurtz and Combet (as the owners then were) made a remarkable Cabernet in the late

60s, forward looking in its skilful use of new oak. A bottle uncorked while writing these notes showed the wine holding colour, varietal fruit and the lift of new oak.

The vineyard was acquired by its new owners Peter and Clare Dunn, Jerome Winston and Jennifer Meek in 1977. Along with Botobolar and one or two other grape growers, pesticides are banned and working of the soil is kept to a minimum.

Established: 1964.

Address: Gulgong Road, Mudgee, 5 km north of township. (063) 722 258.

Winemaker: Jennifer Meek.

Annual crush: 35 tonnes estate grown; 10 tonnes brought in.

Principal wines/wine styles

Cabernet Sauvignon: Clearly the best wine of the vineyard. The '77 won the trophy for best current vintage dry red at the Hunter Valley Show of that year, and three years later was still an extremely youthful wine of intense varietal character needing many more years to soften and fully open up.

Releases for late 1980 will include the following wines: Chardonnay 1980 (6 months in oak) $3.50. Dry Frontignac 1980 $2.50. Traminer 1980 $3.25. Crouchen 1979 $2.75. Semillon 1979 $2.75. Pinot Noir 1979 $4.50. Cabernet Sauvignon 1978 Bin A718 $3.75.

Cellar door sales/facilities: Open Monday to Saturday 9 am to 5 pm; Sunday noon to 4 pm. Tasting facilities.

Retail distribution: Farmer Brothers Canberra; Victorian Wine Centre, South Melbourne. Mail Orders direct to vineyard welcome: PO Box 130, Mudgee, 2850.

Summary: Small vineyard making an astonishing number of wines, mostly in extremely small quantities using a 100-year-old hand press and a lot of help from friends. Quality is variable.

Murrumbidgee Irrigation Area

Centred on Griffith, but taking in Leeton and Yenda as well, the Murrumbidgee Irrigation Area (MIA) is and always will be the major wine-producing area of NSW. Its history is inextricably bound up with grape-growing in general and with McWilliams in particular. Until 1912, the Riverina was a desolate place, having been classed as uninhabitable by the explorer John Oxley almost a century before. The transformation followed the 1906 Act passed by the New South Wales Parliament, authorizing the construction of the Barren Jack — subsequently 'aboriginalized' to Burrinjuck — Dam. This was to harness the waters of the Murrumbidgee and use them in exactly the same way as the Canadian-born Chaffey brothers had done with the Murray at Mildura 25 years earlier.

As the water arrived in 1912, so did J J McWilliam, purchasing land at Hanwood and establishing 35,000 cuttings. The McWilliam family's vineyard operations were then based at Junee, and the first Hanwood vintage was crushed there. The Hanwood winery was erected in 1917, and a second one at Yenda in 1920.

Much of the development of the MIA has been controlled by the NSW Water Conservation and Irrigation Commission, with the blocks limited to 30 hectares and sold to individuals only. This was an ideal situation for soldier-resettlement after the First World War, and numerous soldiers duly arrived. But chaos resulted with inferior grape types and inadequate or inappropriate agricultural methods used; it took some years for the industry to get properly into stride.

This process was hastened by the arrival of the first wave of Italian immigrants in the 1920s, many of whom came from the winemaking areas around Traviso in the north of Italy and Calabria in the south. With skill and expertise in grape-growing and winemaking, they immediately made their mark.

The second wave of immigrants, also principally from Italy, arrived after the Second World War. Many of the enormous, gleaming and usually ornate winery complexes are tangible evidence of the spectacular success achieved by these new arrivals.

However, there has been a transformation in other ways too,

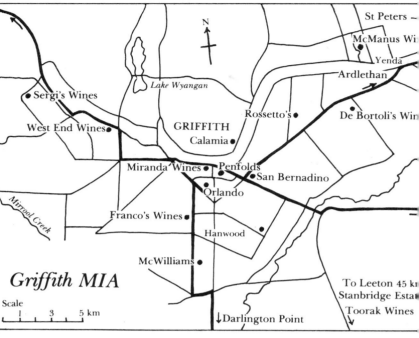

Griffith MIA

Scale
1   3   5 km

this time led by the first arrival in the district: McWilliams. In the 1950s, Glen McWilliam, technical and production director, determined to increase the quality of Riverina wine by both radically improving handling techniques using the newly developed, cooled fermentation process, and by planting superior grape types.

Before this time, it had been assumed that the MIA was suitable only for making heavy sweet and fortified wine. In conjunction with the CSIRO and the Department of Agriculture, the slow process began, and by 1964 the first commercial release was made.

This was a Cabernet Sauvignon which won gold medals at virtually every show, and caused — understandably — a sensation in winemaking circles. At ten years of age it was still drinking superbly, effectively answering the critics who at the time of its release suggested it would be a seven-day wonder. It was followed in 1966 by an equally pretigous Rhine Riesling; Traminer came later and then the veritable cascade of varietals now available.

The top-class McWilliams wines represent some of the best value for money the country has to offer in flavoursome, clean, straightforward drinking. Without doubt, there is no other wine-producing country which produces wines of such quality in such quantity and for so modest a cost.

Others, large and small, have followed McWilliams example, often with direct assistance in the form of cuttings from the top varietals. Stan Aliprandi of San Bernadino is a tireless ambassador for the district, producing a wide range of high-quality varietals and never missing an opportunity to proclaim the ability of the district to produce fine wine.

However, for better or worse, the basic function of the MIA is to provide the enormous quantities of white and red wine destined to fill the casks and flagons which now account for a staggering majority of total wine sales. Why there should be a neurosis about accepting this role I really cannot imagine. Those same casks and flagons dominate the wine market simply because the public sees them as providing wine at its most acceptable price and quality.

Slightly more sensitive, no doubt, is the fact of the vast MIA production of wine concoctions. The wine lists of many of the Italian-owned-and-run wineries look like the figment of a child's imagination: chocmint Marsala has given me the odd nightmare since I saw it on a list.

It seems to me the claims for quality lie firmly in the field of varietal white wines. High yields (14 tonnes to the hectare and upwards) have a very much less marked effect than on red wines, one of the most obvious reasons being the lack of importance of skin colour and flavour in whites. Careful winemaking — with the aid of centrifuges, stabilization and filtration prior to fermentation, controlled temperature fermentation, and early bottling — results in marvellous white wines.

They have extremely fresh fruit flavour, pronounced varietal character, and are soft, rounded wines ready for drinking as soon as they are bottled. With a very few exceptions, these are not wines for cellaring, but neither is French Beaujolais, and few would dispute the rating of that wine as one of the classic wine styles.

CB de Bortoli

Oldest and largest of the family-owned Griffith wineries, de Bortoli is also one of the most cosmopolitan in its outlook. No doubt because it has always been prepared to look beyond the Italian market, and because of large cellaring–wholesale facilities in Sydney, its growth since 1928 (when eight thousand litres were made) has been phenomenal.

It now stores eight million litres and crushes seven thousand tonnes of grapes each year. More than fifty different wines and spirits are produced at the winery, an uncommon practice these days when most sparkling and many fortified wines tend to be bought in from specialist contract makers.

The company produces a wide range of flagon wines and believes that these should be of equal quality to bottled wines. This philosophy is particularly valid against the background of the soft, early-drinking styles which the MIA is so well placed to produce.

Established: 1923.
Address: Yenda Road, Bilbul, 9 km east of Griffith.
Winemaker: Brian Edwards.
Annual crush: 7000 tonnes.

Principal wines/wine styles
It is impossible to do justice to the immense array of wines, and also difficult to accept without prejudice that modern technology coupled with an immense selection of fruit to choose from can, and does, result in some extremely pleasant table wines.
White varietals: Pinot Chardonnay (soft and full, fairly low in acid); Rhine Riesling (fairly light, but clean and finishes very crisp); Semillon (made as a Moselle style with distinct residual sugar); white Burgundy (a full-bodied blend of Semillon, Trebbiano and Gordo).
Red Table Wines: Claret (blend or Shiraz, Mataro and Grenache);

Burgundy (Malbec supplemented by small French and American oak); Shiraz-Troia (full-bodied with good colour).
Fortified Wines: Vintage Ports include straight Cabernet and straight Troia versions.
Spumante: Vittorio Spumante is one of the better wines of its style on the market.
Best buys
Vittorio Spumante: $1.70
Cellaring Potential: Most wines ready to drink when sold.
Cellar door sales/facilities: Open Monday to Saturday 8.30 am to 5.30 pm. Full tasting facilities.
Retail distribution: Griffith and Sydney.
Summary: Large turnover and product range is based upon a combination of technically sound winemaking and excellent value for money.

Franco's Wines

Franco's Wines has its origins in 1933 when the family purchased the fruit farm and vineyard on which the present winery stands. Each year the family made 100 gallons of wines for its own use from grapes grown on the property; in 1959 (in response to requests from relatives and friends) a fruit-packing shed was converted into a winery, and from 1964 the crush was supplemented by grapes bought in from adjoining properties.

The winemaking is in the hands of a consultant, Louis Delpiano, Italian born and qualified. The inevitable melange of wines and related drinks are made, and prices are if anything even lower than other vineyards in the district. A 1970 vintage Claret was still available at $1.60 or $18.00 per dozen at the time of writing. The top red, a 1975 Cabernet Sauvignon Bin 2/48

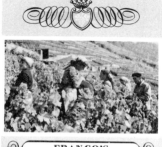

was similarly priced. Many wines offered are non-vintage, being designed for immediate consumption while still fresh.

Established: 1959.

Address: Irrigation Way, Hanwood, 5 km south of Griffith. (069) 621 675.

Winemaker: Louis Delpiano.

Annual Crush: 1200 tonnes.

Principal wines/wine styles

Flagon/bulk and bottled table wines for as little as 55 cents per litre. Flagon/bulk and bottled dessert wines (i.e., fortified), 11 to choose from. Limited range of mature red wines, Muscat and Port. Sparkling wines.

Best buys

Claret 1970: $1.60

Cabernet Sauvignon 1975: $1.60

Reserve Port 1973: $2.20

Cellar door sales/facilities: Open Monday to Saturday 8.30 am to 5.30 am. Italian-style tasting facilities.

Retail distribution: Principally to Italian community, Griffith and Sydney. Cellar door/mail order sales welcome.

Summary: One of the smaller Griffith operations with very low prices an obvious attraction.

CC McManus Wines

If Stanbridge is small by normal MIA standards, McManus is minute. What it lacks in size, however, it more than makes up for in individuality. Dr David McManus is winemaker; Miss Marguerite McManus is manageress and Catherine Marie Bellew cellar mistress. Other members of the family (it is very much a family concern) are Thelmay, Raghnall and John Bruce — these family names appear on the labels of the wines "as they do not fall readily into the normal categories of wines".

This is putting it mildly. McManus' meagre intake of grapes comes from vines which have received far less water than usual, with much reduced yield and far greater colour and fruit flavour. The wines are matured in stainless steel with oak chips added where necessary; 'Catherine Marie' is subjected to a primitive form of pasteurization to produce a very passable sweet red. Quality is extremely variable but all the wines have character.

Established: 1969.

Address: Farm 1347 Yenda, 1 km west of Yenda (PO Box 29 Yenda, 2682). (069) 68 1064.

Winemaker: Dr D B McManus.

Annual crush: 20–40 tonnes.
Annual sales: 500–700 cases.
Principal wines/wine styles
Marguerite: A blend of 70% Semillon; 20% Chardonnay and 10% Trebbiano. Golden colour; immense tropical-fruit-salad bouquet, suggesting sweetness although the wine is in fact quite dry. Big, rich flavour which falls away a little on the finish due to lack of acid.
Pinot Noir: Typical pale Pinot colour. Sweet fruit bouquet and similar palate, suggesting there may be a trace of residual sugar. Recognizable varietal character.
Hermitage Raghnall Bin 2: Medium colour to good. Pleasant fruit flavour held back by hard metallic edge. Clearly deprived of softening effects of normal wood ageing.
Catherine Marie: "Heat-treated Cabernet, rich and black, a cross between a Burgundy and a Port". Winemaker's quotes, but they well describe a most unusual sweet red, which sells very well.

Best buys
1976 Marguerite: $1.50
1976 Catherine Marie: $3.00
1975 Hermitage (Raghnall Bin 2): $1.70
Cellaring potential: Wines are ready for drinking.
Cellar door sales/facilities: Open Monday to Saturday 8.30 am to 5.30 pm; Sunday noon to 5 pm. Tasting facilities.
Retail distribution: Virtually nil. Mail orders/cellar door sales welcome.
Summary: A totally unconventional approach to grape-growing (for the MIA) and winemaking (for anywhere) results in utterly unconventional wines.

103

BA McWilliams Wines

The contribution of McWilliams to the Riverina — indeed to the Australian wine industry as a whole — cannot be overemphasised. It is easy to say that with the largest and longest established wineries in the area, McWilliams was the best positioned to introduce the technical revolution which was to transform the area from a mass producer of rough wine suitable only for fortification into one providing the major part of New South Wales table wine production. The fact is that such radical change seldom comes from a market leader, and all the more credit goes to the foresight and innovation of the McWilliams family led by technical director Glen McWilliam.

To add further lustre to their record, McWilliams have always been active in assisting both government bodies and private growers to share in the benefits of McWilliams own research and development.

The Riverina operations of McWilliams are spread over 4 wineries: Hanwood, Yenda, Beelbangera and (across the river in Victoria) Robinvale.

Hanwood was the first to be erected and in 1917 crushed 170 tonnes: today's capacity is 14,000 tonnes. Total storage capacity is 22.5 million litres, and a significant part of this is in the form of 11,000 oak casks. At the other end of the scale are four 450,000 litre storage tanks and nine stainless steel rail tankers. Hanwood (together with Robinvale) is the main dry table wine production and storage centre.

At Yenda the sparkling Markview champagne is made, a wine which year in, year out provides top value for money in its low price bracket. Other wines are also made at Yenda, including the two brandy stills in operation there.

Beelbangera was the third complex acquired by McWilliams (Robinvale came last, being commenced in 1961), and unlike the other wineries was acquired as a going concern. Its capacity has been much upgraded since, and it makes a considerable part of the fortified wine output of the group. As with all centres, a number of differing wine types and styles are processed.

In continuing witness to McWilliams' willingness to innovate are the Rosedale 2 litre flagons, using a bottle and polystyrene label employed by soft drink makers, and the Clarsac, Valsac and Mos Sac 2 glass wine sachets made from lined plastic.

The principal wines are, of course, the varietal reds and whites and Hanwood Port. In their price range these wines are unbeatable and the quality is extremely consistent from one year to the next.

Established: Hanwood 1917. Yenda 1920. Beelbangera 1900.

Location: Hanwood 1900. Yenda 1900. Beelbangera 1900.
Winemakers: Hanwood: Herb Egger.
Yenda: J J A McWilliam. Beelbangera: Peter Turley.
Annual crush: Hanwood 14,000 tonnes. Yenda 10,000 tonnes.
Beelbangera 8,000 tonnes.

Principal wines/wine styles

Chenin Blanc 1979: One of the best – if not the best – of the '79 varietal releases. Abundant fruit on bouquet and, like the other wines, full flavour on the palate. A soft, generous and easy drinking wine.

Chardonnay 1978: A little of this wine may still be around on retailers shelves. It was one of the best of this line from McWilliams, offering considerable rich Chardonnay flavour yet with sufficient acid to give it balance. The '80 vintage will be on release by the time of publication.

Cabernet Sauvignon 1966: A re-release of this wine gives the opportunity to see one of the greatest Riverina reds fully developed. It has 11 gold medals and the Gilbert Phillips Trophy for best red wine of the 1970 Sydney Show to its credit. The colour is still deep and strong, although with some browning as one would expect. Rather old fashioned style, with roast fruit aroma. A clean wine, however, with lovely mature combination of oak and fruit on the palate.

Best buys

Chenin Blanc 1979: $2.80;Chardonnay 1980: $2.80;Cabernet Sauvignon 1975: $2.80;Cabernet Sauvignon 1966: $5.25.

Cellaring potential: Varietal Whites are at their best on release; some indeed feel McWilliams should market them sooner than they do at present. Reds 4–7+ years, showing great suppleness with age.

Cellar door sales/facilities: *Hanwood*: The famous Hanwood Barrell, a tasting–sales complex fashioned in the shape of an oak cask open Monday to Saturday 9 am to 6 pm. Winery tours 10 am to 2.30 pm Monday to Friday.

Yenda: Small tasting facilities and sales open 9 am to 5 pm Monday to Friday.

Beelbangera: Not open.

Summary: McWilliams white wines are soft, clean, full flavoured styles with ample varietal definition ideal for early drinking.

CB Miranda Wines

Miranda is another of the extraordinary family success stories in the Griffith area. From a foot-crushed first vintage in 1940 by newly arrived Francisco Miranda, it has grown to a multi-million dollar enterprise.

The Miranda family has always been willing to embrace the benefits of new technology. Their installation in 1958 of an ion-exchange column (to lower pH) is claimed to have been the first in Australia; and extensive fermentation-cooling systems are also used to maximize fruit flavour. For many years the winemaker was Ron Potter, the inventor of the world-famous Potter Fermenter, now managing director of his own public company.

Miranda ventured into the sparkling-wine market in 1978, and in the first year of operation 100,000 cases were made, increasing to 150,000 cases in the second year.

Bulk wines have always underpinned the operation, but it has also moved decisively towards producing limited quantities of high-quality table wines and evidence of this is a most interesting 1979 Shiraz made from late-pruned vines.

Established: 1939.

Address: Irrigation Way, Griffith, on southern outskirts of township, (PO Box 405, Griffith, 2680). (069) 62 4033.

Winemaker: Bruce Holm.

Annual crush: 5000 tonnes bought in.

Annual sales: 350,000 cases.

Principal wines/wine styles

The seemingly obligatory, enormous range of sparkling wines, dry whites, dry reds, sweet whites, sweet reds, Vermouths, Marsalas and cocktail nips. The principal lines are Golden Gate Spumantes, charmat-fermented and relying on naturally retained sugar for initial fermentation. Medal winners in national shows.

Riesling: Sold both in bottle and flagon, and yet the '78 version

was a silver medal winner at Brisbane. Fresh, crisp and fruity wine.

Shiraz: 1979 Bin 145 is one of the first commercial releases from very-late-pruned vines. The effect is to delay normal ripening, reduce yields, increase colour and acid and lower pH. It is a costly process and this very good wine is clear evidence of Miranda's commitment to quality.

Cellar door sales/facilities: Open Monday to Saturday 8.30 am to 5.30 pm. Enormous sales area called Uncle Sam's Liquor Barn. A trolly supermarket offering a bewildering array of cut-price wines, spirits and beers.

Retail distribution: Through large discount shops in capital cities.

Summary: A technically very strong producer backed up aggressive marketing with a growth pattern second to none.

San Bernadino

Due partly to the drive of the ubiquitous Stan Aliprandi (part-owner) and partly to skilled winemaking, San Bernadino stands unchallenged as the source of the finest dry table and sparkling wines in the Griffith area. Aliprandi is an ambassador-at-large for the Griffith area as a whole, determined to disprove the reputation the district has as a cheap bulk producer of rough reds and whites by Italians for Italians.

Output of San Bernadino rocketed upwards between '73 and '75 from 35,000 dozen to 100,000 dozen. More importantly, however, Brian Croser was retained as a consultant for the '75 vintage and shaped the future direction of the company. Since that time it has concentrated on producing varietals which faithfully reflect the flavour of the grapes from which they are made.

San Bernadino has been spectacularly successful in this endeavour. Its '79s are, without exception, excellent wines, from the refreshing lemony tang of the Rhine Riesling to the fleshy,

'Trout' Trebbiano, to the full, rich and aromatic Traminer, to the round and smooth white Sauvignon.

The dry-white table wines have received wide acceptance, but the success of their sparkling wines has been even more remarkable. The San Bernadino Gran Spumante is one of the best cheap sparkling wines made in Australia today. It is a clean, fresh wine with just the right amount of sweet Muscat fruit flavour. San Bernadino makes a bewildering array of wine cocktails of every shape and hue including non-alcoholic grape drinks.

Established: 1973.

Address: Leeton Road, Griffith, on southern fringe of township. (069) 62 1391.

Winemaker: Scott Collett.

Annual crush: 1000 tonnes estate grown; 9000 tonnes bought in.

Annual sales: 800,000 cases.

Principal wines/wine styles

There are over 100 different table and fortified wines on the San Bernadino list. But the real interest for the wine-lover lies in the 16 varietal whites, 3 varietal red and older vintage private bin dry reds.

Space does not permit a comprehensive review of such a wide range, but the Rhine Riesling, Traminer, Sauvignon Blanc, Trebbiano, and (usually) Chardonnay stand out. Other seldom-marketed varietals such as Golden Chasselas, Marsanne and Frontignan Blanc add further interest.

Most of the old private-bin dry reds have won numerous show awards, and while not entirely escaping the limitations of their birthplace, are soft and pleasant wines.

108

The Gran Spumante is one of the leading sparkling wines on the market today, offering exceptional value for money.

Best buys
Traminer A14 1979: $2.50
Rhine Riesling 1979: $2.50
Cabernet Shiraz 195 1974: $4.00
Gran Spumante NV: $2.25
Cellaring potential: Marketed when ready to drink.
Cellar door sales/facilities: Open Monday to Saturday 8.30 am to 5.30 pm. Extensive tasting facilities. Cellar door/mail order sales.
Summary: San Bernadino shows just what can be achieved in the Griffith area, producing distinctive and extremely attractive varietal whites and excellent sparkling wines.

Sergi's Wines

A long, in-line winery, built in tasteful feature-brick in Hispano—Griffith architectural style, was completed in 1975, and is as striking as the publicity its owners have recently received in other quarters. Somewhat unusually, the winery concentrates on dry table wines rather than fortified styles, which is a welcome change. Just as unusually, the emphasis is on dry reds rather than dry whites. A range of both vintage and non-vintage reds is offered, all at very low prices and all of the soft, drink-now style.
Established: 1971.
Address: Hillston Road, Griffith, 12 km west of township. (069) 62 4122.
Winemaker: L Delpiano (consultant).
Annual crush: 2500 tonnes.
Principal wines/wine styles
Riesling (Semillon-Trebbiano blend).
Moselle (Semillon-Trebbiano-Sultana).
Claret-Hermitage.
Cabernet Sauvignon.
Cellar door sales/facilities: Open Monday to Saturday 8.30 am to 5 pm.
Retail distribution: Virtually nil; cellar door sales to local custom.
Summary: A medium-sized winery concentrating on soft, easy-drinking, cheap red wines.

Stanbridge Estate

It comes as something of a culture shock to find a Griffith

winery with an annual crush of 20 tonnes and no desire to ever increase this past 50 tonnes. Roger Hoare is Australian-born with a mixed vineyard–orchard operation, and runs his winery with his wife. He takes the enterprise seriously, however, having obtained a diploma in oenology from the Riverina College of Advanced Education.

Hoare concentrates on the production of white varietals, and released a 1979 vintage of Semillon, Sauvignon Blanc, Rhine Riesling and a highly unusual Chardonnay Traminer blend. The latter wine, with a trace of residual sugar, was the pick of the range.

Established: 1977.
Address: 10 km west of Leeton on main Griffith–Leeton Highway (farm 1773, Stanbridge, 2705).
Winemaker: Roger Hoare.
Annual crush: 20 tonnes.

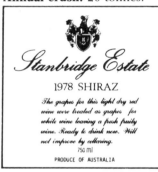

Principal wines/wine styles
Traminer: Usually made with some residual sugar. Fresh, light and spicy.
Rhine Riesling: Fermented dry, crisp and clear.
Chardonnay/Traminer 1979: A highly unusual blend, and to complete the confusion, has a little sugar. Fruity oak and aromatic with the Traminer dominant. Nice wine but tends to cloy a bit on the finish.
Cabernet Sauvignon: Typical light varietal fruit flavour filled out by maturation for 18 months in French oak.
Sauvignon Blanc 1979: Typical Sauvignon Blanc bouquet when made dry; fairly muted. Good palate, excellent acid on finish (particularly given the area) and good fruit. Appealing wine.
Cellar door sales: Open Monday to Saturday 10 am to 6 pm; Sunday noon to 4 pm.
Cellaring potential: Ready to drink on release.
Retail distribution: Very limited, Great Australian Wine Company, 39a Willoughby Road, Crows Nest, Sydney.

110

Best buys
Sauvignon Blanc: $2.40
Sauvignon Traminer: $2.40
Summary: A miniscule operation among the giants of Griffith, with its own quite separate approach to winemaking and quality control.

St Peters

St Peters Distillery Pty Limited, its full name, was established in 1978 by Count Felice Sassoli d' Bianchi and his son Count Andrea Sassoli d' Bianchi. Its ultra-modern and very large winery is attractively landscaped with the maximum retention of native gums and is very different in feeling from most Griffith wineries — the emphasis is on functional design from start to finish.
Established: 1978.
Address: St Peters Road, off Whitton Stock Route, 8 km east of Yenda. (069) 68 1303.
Winemakers: Michael Rohan; Enrico Lavagnino.
Annual crush: 800 tonnes bought in.
Principal wines/wine styles:
Brandy: Quality yet to be revealed.
Cellar door sales/facilities: None at time of writing, but planned for the future.
Retail distribution: Castle Wines and Buton Australia Pty. Limited (Sydney); European Foods (Perth); Miguel Salerno (Adelaide).
Summary: A lavishly equipped venture which intends to concentrate in the toughest and most over-supplied market of all — Australian brandy. If the quality is there, the product should sell, however.

Toorak Wines

Toorak wines have grown steadily since founded by Frank and Vince Bruno in 1963. The company produces a full range of wines from bulk table wines (at 55 cents a litre) to an impressive range of Marsalas, Vermouths and cocktails ($1.30 a bottle or 90 cents a litre in bulk) to sparkling wines including the irresistible Sip-n-go Streaking (a mere $1.40 a bottle, never mind a sip) then to private-bin reds and whites ($1.90 to $2.00 a bottle).

Considerable care and modern technology are applied to the maturing of the whites and the resulting wines are clear and with obvious varietal character. The private bin Cabernet Sauvignon is the best of the reds; although on the light side, it has good acid and will stand cellaring.

Established: 1963.

Address: Toorak Road, Leeton, 4 km west of township. (069) 532523.

Winemaker: Frank Bruno.

Annual crush: 300 tonnes estate grown; 1200 tonnes bought in.

Annual sales: 650,000 litres.

Principal wines/wine styles

Rhine Riesling: Fruit selected from Stoney Point Vineyard and cold-fermented. Good varietal bouquet and flavour.

Riesling Bin 27: Made from Semillon.

White Burgundy Bin 58: Made from Trebbiano, full-flavoured, round and soft.

Cabernet Sauvignon Bin 88: Matured in American Oak and picked with a little more acid than usual.

Best buys

1979 Rhine Riesling: $2.00

1975 Cabernet Sauvignon Bin 88: $2.00

Cellar door sales/facilities: Open 9 am to 6 pm Monday to Saturday. Tasting facilities.

Retail distribution: Limited Sydney and Melbourne.

Summary: Toorak offers a wide range of very inexpensive wines which sell well to the Italian communities in Melbourne and Sydney as well as Griffith/Leeton.

DC West End Wines

Brothers Bill (winemaker) and Tony (sales manager) Calabria took over the winery in 1968, twenty years after it was first opened by their father. Until five years ago all the output was sold in bulk, but increasing amounts are sold in bottle and flagon.

In common with other wineries in the district, it produces a kaleidoscopic range of table and fortified wines and wine de-

West End
Private Bin

BIN No. T.36
GRAPE VARIETY Traminer/Rhine Riesling
YEAR 1979
LITRES 1860

WINEMAKERS COMMENTS

This blend of premium varietal wine
was harvested & fermented in one vat.
The marriage of these two grapes has
enhanced their varietal character while
retaining a full Traminer finish.

WEST END WINES, GRIFFITH

750 mI PRODUCT OF AUSTRALIA   D2950

West End
Moselle

Produced and Bottled by
WEST END WINES, GRIFFITH – N.S.W.
PRODUCT OF AUSTRALIA   750 ml   D2950

rivatives — a flagon of Chocmint Marsala at $2.85 being one of the choicer offerings on the price list.

However, Bill Calabria does make a serious and successful effort to make high-quality table wines, Ports and Sherries. Most of these come from Calabria's own nineteen-hectare vineyard and have been consistent prize winners at recent Griffith wine shows.

Established: 1948.

Address: Braynes Road, Griffith, 2 km west of township (farm 1283, Griffith, 2680). (069) 622868.

Winemaker: Bill Calabria.

Annual crush: 430 tonnes.

Annual sales: 148,000 litres (bulk and bottled).

Principal wines/wine styles

The comprehensive range of table and fortified wines makes its appearance, and indeed it has only been in recent years that West End have moved away from selling virtually all their wine in bulk.

White Varietals: Based on freshness and fruit retention with a conscious effort to retain balancing acid.

Dry Reds: Smooth, with soft and clean finish designed to emphasise fruit flavour.

Bettina Port: Ruby style Port made from very ripe grapes (15 Baume) resulting in strong fruit flavour and clean finish.

Cellar door sales/facilities: Open Monday to Saturday 8.30 am to 5.30 pm; Sunday noon to 5 pm. Full tasting facilities; winery inspections welcome. BBQ facilities.

Retail distribution: Coogee Bay Hotel, Toongabbie Liquor Shop, Villawood Cellars (NSW).

Summary: The accent is on value for money, but the '79 Trebbiano Rhine Riesling is a more than acceptable bin wine as is the Bettina Port fortified range.

Other Districts

The early history of vine-growing and winemaking in New South Wales saw vineyards planted at Bathurst, Camden, Inverell and many other places of which few if any records survive. The proliferation of the past twenty years only goes part of the way to restoring the balance, and I have no doubt that if I were writing this book in twenty years time this section would be significantly larger.

Thus the late Maurice O'Shea made some marvellous Junee whites and reds in the late '40s and early '50s; Oberon has a climate extraordinarily similar to that of Macon in the south of Burgundy; an acquaintance of mine is starting planting vines on his property near Goulburn; I believe Murray Tyrrell has recently planted Rhine Riesling in the hills near Armidale. Although we cannot really claim them as ours, there are a considerable number of vignerons with small plantings around Canberra. (Indeed, eight years ago my Brokenwood partners and I planted an acre of grapes on a property near Bungendore, a venture defeated by an abnormal drought, errant cows and the logistics of absentee ownership rather than by any want of suitability in the carefully chosen, frost-free slope.)

The districts covered in this section are an unqualified potpourri, and the motivations and justifications of the founding vignerons are many and varied. It is, however, not overly fanciful to see in many a reincarnation of the pioneering spirit which was so important to Australia in the last century and which led to so many deeds and discoveries impossible by today's standards.

The courage, ingenuity and perseverance of those pioneers is no less important today to the vigneron who establishes (or re-establishes) a vineyard in a virgin area. He can only guess how the varieties he selects will respond to the climate; when they grow, the birds descend in their multitudes; when the wine is made there is no one he can turn to for advice at critical moments.

As many of the winemakers in these new areas are enthusiastic amateurs with no formal training, this last disability is frequently the most significant. In my first three or four years of winemaking, the passing comment and quick word of advice from Murray Tyrrell, Gerry Sissingh, Max Lake and others calling through (or, in extremes, summoned) was worth its weight in gold. There is no winemaker worth two bob who thinks he knows it all, and is not ever willing to show his new wines, swap notes and give and seek advice from his fellow vignerons.

That advice must be given before it is too late, and at vintage time hours can be too long; even thereafter, delay in administering one treatment or another to a wine in cask may be critical. So if some of the wines from these out-of-the-way weekend operations are less than perfect (and some of them clearly are) it is hardly surprising. Allowances can and should be made and the hope is that, with time, many of the blemishes will disappear.

The most promising districts are those with cooler ripening conditions, and in most instances this is due to altitude. Young and Inverell are obvious examples, with vintage stretching into late April. They have the added advantage of a normally dry and mould-free late summer—early autumn, something which certainly cannot be said for the Hunter Valley.

No doubt we will hear more from such areas, and others like them, in the not-too-distant future. Both the State Department of Agriculture and the various wine schools (Roseworthy and Wagga) are becoming increasingly skilled in the complexities of vineyard-site selection. With the use of sophisticated, computer-based overlay technology, a mass of data is being built up which will not only push the horizons further back, but make the process of doing so a great deal less uncertain than it was.

CB Barwang

The Barwang vineyards are situated 23 km south-east of Young at an elevation of about 500 metres. Very cool, very dry ripening conditions (the 800 mm rainfall is concentrated in winter and spring) means the fruit is harvested in April (compared with the Hunter's February), almost invariably in perfect condition.

With other outposts such as Inverell, Wellington, Canberra and Cowra, it seems we have barely scratched the surface of the potential vineyard areas of New South Wales. It is a lonely business, however, producing wine in an area in which you are one of a handful of vignerons particulary if – as usually happens – you are self-taught. Peter Robertson at Barwang seems to have surmounted these problems with some help from the Riverina College of Advanced Education wine school, and is making some very interesting wines of great flavour. There is no question about the potential of the area.

Established: 1975.

Address: Barwang Road, Young, 23 km south-east of township. (063) 822 689.

Winemaker: Peter Robertson.

Annual crush: 20–40 tonnes estate grown, 1 tonne bought in.

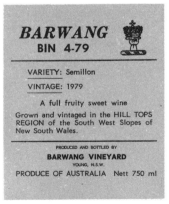

Principal wine/wine styles

Semillon Bin 6 1979: Semillon which performs much more in style of Rhine Riesling, no doubt due to the cool climate. Fresh wine; quite distinct residual sugar gives a touch of sweetness to the middle palate. Finishes crisp.

Semillon Bin 4 1979: Intense flavour; builds immediately the wine is taken into the mouth although the finish is not so long. Very interesting style which should come on very well in the bottle. Both wines show strong yeast influence.

Shiraz Cabernet 1977: Immense purple-blue colour. Mint backed by spice in complex fruit bouquet. Huge fruit–spice flavour marred by hard acid finish. May soften given time; I do not know.

Shiraz Bin 12 1978: Intense colour, but slightly lighter than 1977s. A very big wine which again has a touch of hardness along with enormous flavour and extract.

Vintage Port 78: Some oxidation on bouquet, very pleasant, powerful fruit palate. Very big wine.

Best buys: 1979 Semillon Bin 4: $3.00

1979 Semillon Bin 6: $3.00

1977 Shiraz Cabernet: $2.10

1978 Vintage Port: $5.00

Cellaring potential: Semillon, 2–5+ years; Shiraz Cabernet, 5–8+ years; vintage Port, 6–10 years.

Cellar door sales/facilities: Open 9 am to 12 noon and 1 pm to 5 pm, Monday to Saturday. Tasting and BBQ facilities.

Retail distribution: University House, Canberra, ACT.

Summary: White, red and fortified wines all distinguished by a rarely encountered deepness and intensity of flavour. Some balance problems with the reds which bottle age may cure, but earlier picking might have partly forestalled.

Ϗ Camden Bridge Farm

Norman Hanckel was a member of the famous Roseworthy class of 1946–47, graduating in agriculture. For many years he was General Manager and then a Director of Hungerford Hill Limited before moving on to the Industries Assistance Commission in 1979.

In 1974 he began a vineyard at Camden on the banks of the Nepean River, more or less opposite the site of Macarthur's Vineyards established over 150 years before — vineyards which at the time were the most extensive in New South Wales.

Until the 1980 vintage, the grapes were sold to Hungerford Hill, but in that year Bridge Farm crushed 80 tonnes of grapes and produced its first wines. Cool nights result in a vintage at least four weeks later than the Hunter Valley, and very fruity whites and soft, full-flavoured reds are produced.

Established: 1974.

Address: Lot 3, Macarthur Road, Camden, 2570. (046) 668 3377.

Winemaker: Norman Hanckel.

Annual crush: 80 tonnes.

Principal wines/wine styles

Will eventually encompass the main varieties planted of

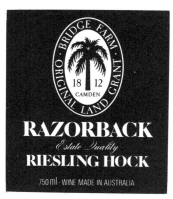

Traminer, Chardonnay, Trebbiano, Rhine Riesling, Shiraz and Cabernet Sauvignon.

Premium release of estate-grown-and-produced wines: "Bridge Farm Camden" Trebbiano and "Bridge Farm Camden" Riesling/Traminer. Second range will be released with the "Bridge Farm — Razorback" label under generic Burgundy, Moselle etc., labels.

Cellar door sales/facilities: Not established at time of writing but planned for the future and may be available later in 1980.

Retail distribution: Distributed through Bulmer's Cider at Campbelltown.

Summary: It will be fascinating to watch the results of history repeating itself.

CX Chisletts Wines

A small, family-run winery which has been quietly making and selling wines for many years now, but which is virtually unheard of in Sydney and interstate. (Also known as Lachlan Valley Wines.)

The inland central western slopes area — centred on the triangle formed by Cowra, Young and Forbes — proves its potential as a wine-growing area by the quality of the fruit produced. The basic fruit flavour in the Chislett Wines is very good and after some early problems with volatility in the reds, the wines have won a number of medals at both regional and national wine shows.

Address: Wandary Lane, Forbes, 6 km from township (063) 521028.

Winemakers: F P & L A Chislett.

Annual crush: 20–40 tonnes.

Principal wines/wine styles

Semillon 1979: Full-bodied, dry.

Shiraz 1977: Clean, full-flavoured. Bronze medal winner, Sydney Show 1978.

Cabernet Sauvignon 1977: Robust wine with good varietal flavour. Winner of several regional wine show medals.

Vintage Port 1978: Made from Cabernet and (of all things) Pinot Noir.

Cellar door sales/facilities: Open 9 am to 5.30 pm Monday to Saturday; Sunday 1 pm to 5 pm. Tasting facilities only.

Retail distribution: Nil.

Summary: Output is very limited and the winery caters exclusively to local trade, but the quality is there to justify a wider audience.

X Cogno Brothers

A little bit of Italy comes to Cobbitty, on the northern side of Camden, where brothers John and Dino Cogno make a considerable amount of wine, principally from grapes purchased in South Australia. The output of the winery is heavily directed towards Italian clientele. Their own plantings are centred on the classic Italian variety Barbera, and all wines made have some residual sugar.

Established: 1964.

Address: Cobbitty Road, Cobbitty, 8 km north-west of Camden. (046) 51 2281.

Winemakers: John and Dino Cogno.

Principal wines/wine styles

Barbera: Sweet red table wines.

Sparkling Spumantes: Sweet.

Summary: Wines made in a particular style for a particular clientele; a recipe for sure success.

B Cubbaroo

Cubbaroo Wines really defy all the normal precepts about the production of quality dry red wines. There is simply no way that wines with a haunting echo of St Emilion or Pomerol in France should come from the flat rich black soil plains in the irrigated cotton and wheat belt of the Namoi Valley of inland northern New South Wales. Right from the first vintage in '73, reaching — so far — a highpoint in '74, the reds have shown very good flavour and balance, and have won 30 medals in national shows from reasonably restricted outings. Forty hectares are under vine, and red, rose and white wines are made.

Established: 1970.
Address: Narrabri-Walgett Highway near Burren Junction.
Winemaker: Brian McGuigan (Wyndham Estate).
Annual crush: 600 tonnes.

Principal wines/wine styles
Shiraz: A curious combination of rich fruit and leafy herbaceous flavours — hot and cold climates all wrapped up together. Authentic and individual wines which deserve to be taken seriously and do not need to rely on the unexpected location of the vineyard as a sales gimmick.
Dry White: Full flavoured fairly broad style for early drinking.
Moselle: Conventional.
Rose: Acceptable.

Best Buys
Shiraz '76: $2.65
Dry White '79: $2.95
Cellaring potential: Whites and Roses drink now; Shiraz 4–7 years.
Cellar door sales/facilities: Open 8 am to 6 pm Monday to Saturday. Barbecue facilities.
Retail distribution: In NSW, Hunter Valley Wine Co.
Summary: Opens up yet another dimension to winemaking in New South Wales and produces some of the best reds from the "other areas".

D'Aquino Winery

A winery which is as much a wine shop, which secures its fruit from such diverse places as Hillstone and Corowa, and which rather surprisingly sits on the Mitchell Highway on the outskirts of Orange. Much of the production is of fortified wine and most of this is in turn bought in from other wineries. However, the youngest of the D'Aquino family is at Roseworthy and the future may well see greater emphasis placed on table wines.

Established: 1949.

Address: Cnr. Mitchell Highway & Cox Avenue, Orange, on north-western outskirts of town. (063) 627 381.

Winemaker: Leo D'Aquino.

Principal wines/wine styles

Several dry reds (Shiraz, Cabernet) and dry whites (Rhine Riesling, Semillon) of acceptable quality. Extensive fortified wine list, much of it bought in.

Cellar door sales/facilities: Open Monday to Saturday 9.30 am to 8 pm.

Retail distribution: Nil.

Summary: Caters exclusively for district and a small amount of tourist trade.

Gilgai

As any student of history knows, it is forever repeating itself. So it was entirely fitting that Dr Keith Whish should procure his vine cuttings from Dalwood in the Hunter Valley when establishing his vineyard in 1968. 'Re-establishing' would be a better word, for in 1849, Charles Dalwood took vines from Dalwood along with sheep and cattle and ventured north to Inverell to establish Bukkulla Station. This was the outermost settlement in New South Wales at that time and the vines were kept alive during the long journey by being dipped in each creek and river he passed on the way.

Bukkulla was a major wine-producer between 1850 and 1890, supplying much of the wine for which Dalwood was to become world famous. They were reputedly immense wines in colour and body; looking at the new generation Gilgai reds there is no reason to doubt this. At an elevation of 800 metres, the red laterite soil and cool ripening conditions produce wines of exceptional colour and power.

Established: 1968.

Address: Gilgai, 10 km south of Inverell on Tingha Road PO Box 462, Inverell, 2360 . (067) 22 3078.

Winemaker: Dr K M Whish and sons.

Annual crush: 30 tonnes estate grown.

Principal wines/wine styles

Varietal Whites: Trebbiano, Semillon and Rhine Riesling. Interesting wines, but some show the problems involved in handling very small quantities of wine.

Varietal Reds: Cabernet Sauvignon, Shiraz, Shiraz Cabernet, Malbec, Grenache and Mataro. These are very much more appealing. There are few if any problems in making red wine in small quantities.

The pick of the reds are:

Cabernet Shiraz '75: Good colour of medium depth holding its acid well. Pleasant fruit–oak combination on bouquet; pepper-spice tang to fruit flavour; nice acid finish.

Malbec '77: Immense deep-purple colour; chalky, dusty bouquet. Big, deep tannic palate with distinct Bordeaux overtones.

Best buys

1975 Cabernet Shiraz: $2.50

1977 Malbec: $3.00

1976 Mataro: $2.50

Cellaring potential: Whites seemingly limited; reds 3–7+ years, more for the Malbec.

Cellar door sales/facilities: Open 10 am to 6 pm Monday to Saturday; noon to 6 pm Sunday. Tasting, BBQ and picnic facilities.

Retail distribution: Great Australian Wine Co (Sydney). Principally cellar door and mail order inquiries welcome.

Summary: Inverell has a proud history of winemaking and its cool ripening conditions are ideally suited to the production of high-quality wines. It cannot be long before others follow in the path of Dr Whish.

Glenfinlass

If the medical profession supplies many of the part-time winemakers, the legal profession is not far behind. On rich red volcanic soils around Wellington, one of the smallest commercial vineyards in New South Wales produces a small range of dry red table wines. Winemaker and owner is Wellington solicitor Brian Holmes, who retires each weekend to his winery at Elysian Farm.

The tiny output is all sold locally at impressively low prices. The wines are in fact surprisingly good — surprising given the remoteness of the district and the fact that there are (so far) no other vineyards or wineries in the district. The wines are all 'hand made'; natural yeasts only are used; wines are fermented in open tanks with hand plunging; the wine is fined but not filtered prior to bottling. There is, as one would expect, some vintage variation but Brian Holmes says that in typical years the reds are big wines in the Mudgee style.

Address: Elysian Farm, Parkes Road, Wellington. Phone Wellington 1 or 8 (or 221, home).

Winemaker: Brian Holmes.

Annual crush: 14 tonnes estate grown.

Annual sales: 500 cases.

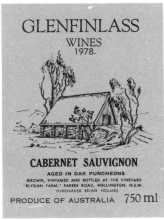

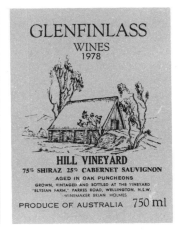

Principal wine/wine styles

Shiraz: Shows vintage variation. '77 vintage was light and extremely elegant, with medium body and crisp finish (bronze medal winner, Mudgee). The '78 was much riper, with a slightly roast character to the fruit.

Shiraz Cabernet: From the Hill Vineyard. Very deep colour, strong purple-blue. Big tannic wine with considerable extract suggesting addition of pressings. Some volatility. Needs much time.

Best buys: 1978 Hill vineyard Shiraz Cabernet: $2.50
1977 Cabernet Sauvignon: $1.50

Cellaring potential: Depends very much on style. '77 Shiraz more or less ready; other reds 3–5+ years.

Cellar door sales/facilities: Open Saturday 10 am to 4 pm and by appointment.

Retail distribution: Nil.

Summary: Some wines technically very well made, others with a few faults, which is hardly surprising. Fruit quality is good.

XC Jasper Valley Wines

One of the newest and certainly the most unusually located vineyards and wineries nestling in the Shoalhaven Valley about 120 kilometres south of Sydney. The vineyards are planted to Rhine Riesling, Chardonnay, Semillon, Shiraz and Cabernet Sauvignon. Vintage occurs in late February, and apart from the necessity for more spraying than usual to combat mould induced by the relatively high rainfall, there are few problems with the climate.

Mr Mitchell learned his winemaking from the Riverina College of Advanced Education and has been helped and advised by Edgar Riek, the well-known Canberra wine identity.

Established: 1976.

Address: Croziers Road, Berry, 5 km south of township. (044) 22960.

Winemaker: S. Mitchell.

Annual crush: 15 tonnes estate grown (1980).

Principal wines/wine styles

Semillon Chardonnay 1979: Some volatility and extractive skin character on bouquet and palate. Reasonable fruit flavour and certainly not undrinkable.

Private Bin Semillon AJ5/79 1979: An eminently acceptable wine of conventional flavour and structure apart from a curious but not unpleasant earthy aroma on bouquet. Soft, fruity palate.

Cellaring potential: Drink now.

Best buys: Private Bin Semillon AJ5/79: $2.30

Cellar door sales/facilities: Open Monday to Saturday 9 am to 5 pm; Sunday noon to 5 pm. Full tasting facilities (single bottle licence).

Retail distribution: Nil.

Summary: The first winery to open in the South Coast area with sales exclusively to Wollongong South Coast clientele. Quality has obvious potential.

⟨ Markeita Cellars

Probably the most obscure vineyard in New South Wales, located in a country town between Molong and Wellington which many people will never have even heard of, let alone visited — Neurea. The vineyards were originally planted exclusively to table grapes for the dried fruit trade, but limited quantities of wine grapes were added later. Highly distinctive fortified wines are the main output.

Established: 1950.

Address: Mitchell Highway, Neurea, 2742. South of Wellington.

Winemaker: R. Reinhard.

Principal wines/wine styles: Unusual fortified and the occasional table wine.

Cellar door sales/facilities: Open Monday to Saturday 8 am to 8 pm; Sunday noon to 6 pm.

Retail distribution: Limited, some in Brisbane.

Summary: Small and virtually unknown winery.

⟩ Mildura Vineyard Wines

Mildura Vineyards is little known in NSW, but has significant distribution in Victoria and is a sizeable operation by any standards. It produces a full range of wines, many of which are (judging by the labels) directed at the considerable tourist traffic passing through Mildura. Offerings such as "Blue Party Girl — a delicate, fruity, bubbly moselle" and "Red Cliffs Big Lizzie — gordo moselle" should not obscure the fact that a number of wines are of National show standard. These include a multiple award winning '76 Cabernet Shiraz, various medal winning Ruby Ports and a Cream Sherry which received a silver medal in 1979 in the toughest school of them all — Rutherglen Show. Top class in Vermouths are also produced.

Address: Silver City Highway, 4 km north-west of Mildura (Box 109, Buronga, 2648). (050) 23 1834.

Winemakers: D Cooper; J R Pollock (consultant).

Annual crush: 700 tonnes estate grown; 300 tonnes bought in.

Annual sales: 500,000 cases.

Principal wines/wine styles

A comprehensive range of dry white and red table wines, for-

MILDURA VINEYARD
MURRAY RIVER PADDLECADE

P.S. MELBOURNE

CABERNET SHIRAZ
CLARET
1976
PRODUCE OF AUSTRALIA
750ml
GROWN, MADE
AND BOTTLED ON THE ESTATE   D 4215
Sydney Show 1977   **SILVER MEDAL**   Class 53
Melbourne Show 1977 **BRONZE MEDAL**   Class 47
Canberra Show 1978 **SILVER MEDAL**   Class 39

ROYAL ADELAIDE SHOW
SILVER
MEDAL
CLASS 9
1976

Blue Party Girl
A delicate fruity bubbly wine
MILDURA VINEYARD WINES   750ml
CARBONATED WINE PRODUCE OF AUSTRALIA
GROWN, MADE & BOTTLED ON THE ESTATE   D4/15

tified and sparkling wines available in bottle, flagon and bulk.
Cabernet Shiraz: '76 was a consistent silver medal winner at
national shows and a gold medal winner at Canberra.
Cabernet Sauvignon: Also of top quality.
Best buys
Bulk wines (less than $1 per litre).
Cabernet Shiraz: $1.70.
Cabernet Sauvignon: $1.50
Ruby Port: $1.35
Prices current February/March 1980 cellar door.
Cellar door sales/facilities: Open 10 am to 6 pm Monday to
Saturday.
Retail distribution: Nil.
Summary: The most expensive wines on the extensive list sells
for less than $1.50 when bought by the dozen, or $1.70 by the
bottle. While Sultana-Gordo Moselle blends are enormously
popular, some good dry red and fortified wines are made.

AA Richmond Estate Vineyard

It is unusual to find new vineyards being established on the
outer fringes of Sydney: the trend both here and in Adelaide is
usually the other way. Penfolds' Rooty Hill vineyard has had the
death sentence hanging over its head for some years now. In
December 1967 Sydney orthopaedic surgeon Barry Bracken
purchased a North Richmond grazing and orchard property,
and in 1968 planted 6 acres of grapes. Over the next 3 years all
failed. For some obscure reason grafted vines proved unsuit-
able and all the vines are now direct producers — a hazardous
situation as phylloxera has appeared previously in the Sydney
metropolitan area.

There are now 22 acres of vineyard dating from the '71 and
later plantings. Roughly half is Cabernet, half Shiraz with some

Malbec and Merlot. While Dr (or Mr, as surgeons are known) Bracken regards a Cabernet/Shiraz/Malbec blend as the definitive vineyard style, easily the most distinguished wine so far made is a '75 Shiraz, which has won gold medals between 1975 and 1979. Production has increased markedly since 1976: from 4,550 litres in that year to over 18,000 litres in 1979.

Established: 1967.
Address: Gadds Road, North Richmond, off Kurmond Road, 3 km from North Richmond township.
Winemaker: Barry Bracken.
Annual crush: 30 tonnes.

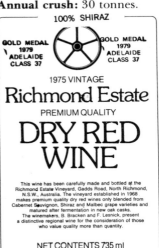

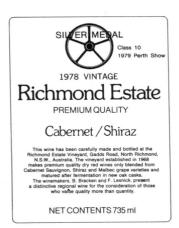

Principal wines/wine styles
Shiraz 1975: exceptional colour retention for a 5 year old hermitage — excellent red — purple clean acidity and beautifully handled oak. Familiar spice to fruit flavour rounds off a high class wine which richly deserves all the medals it has won. Has many, many years in front of it.

Best buys
1977 Cabernet: $2.50
1978 Cabernet Shiraz Malbec: $2.50
Cellaring potential: Shiraz 6–10+ years.
Cellar door sales/facilities: Open Monday to Saturday 9 am to 5 pm.
Retail distribution: Very limited. Crows Nest Cellars, Sydney have limited stocks.
Summary: A virtually unheard of winery until recently, but increased production of high quality reds will inevitably change all that. Yet another successful combination of vine and scalpel.

Index